Qualified to

Reign

Memoirs of a Resilient Queen

ISBN-13: 9781658775007

Publisher's Note

This book is dedicated to every
woman who desires to bounce back
after defeat with their crown intact.
May you continue to reign,
resiliently.

Table of Contents

Introduction

So many women struggle with finding their inner queen because of the past they've experienced. Life can be cruel, and people will make you feel as though you're unworthy of receiving what God has created you to receive. We tend to forget that it's our birthright to be successful, happy, and prosperous. In 1 Peter 2:9, the Bible tells us that we're a part of a royal priesthood, chosen by God. Women tend to forget this because they've lost their crown. It's time to get it back. Despite the journey you've gone through, sis, you're STILL chosen by God and you're STILL Qualified to Reign!

Qualified to Reign: Memoirs of a Resilient Queen is a collection of stories written by powerful women who have allowed God to mold them into a new vessel, remove their residue, and position them on their own God-ordained thrones. Every woman has a past, and a divine assignment. It's our responsibility to heal, grow, and evolve into the woman capable of sitting on her throne. And the co-authors are stepping into their power and showing women how to do the same.

Each contributing writer transparently shares her experience of hitting rock bottom, seeking God for healing, and becoming the woman she was created to be.

After reading each story, you will learn that like the contributing writer, that your past does not disqualify your from experiencing the fullness of God and that you too are a queen who's qualified to reign.

Refined for His Glory

Written by Jessica LeeAnn

That is why, for Christ's sake, I delight in weaknesses, in insults, in hardships, in persecutions, in difficulties. For when I am weak, then I am strong.

2 Corinthians 12:10

It always amazes me when I work with clients and they tell me how professional and patient I am. Whenever I hear this, I immediately give God glory. There was a time in my life that people would refer to me as loud, ghetto, and ratchet. And those descriptions of me were befitting. That's who I was for *many*, many years. Oh, how I thank God for growth!

While today some people may think of me as patient, professional, and purposeful – that wasn't always the case for me. It took me a long time to acquire these traits because I didn't see myself as a woman capable of being patient, professional, or purposeful.

Growing up in Richmond, CA taught me how to be tough. Being loud was a defense mechanism that worked well for me. I was known for having a big mouth, a negative attitude, and for talking a lot of smack. I'm not proud of this reputation, however, I avoided getting into a lot of fights because of this impression of me.

It took me a *long* time to realize that having a big mouth wasn't cute. It's not something that people close to me informed me of, although I'm sure they talked about me behind my back about my big mouth and bad attitude. I found out the hard way that my mouth and my attitude was an issue.

Truth Hurts

My big mouth and negative attitude continued to be an issue for me as I entered young adulthood. After I gave birth to my daughter and navigated through my 20's – it actually became worse. My attitude caused me to lose my best friend, created tension within my family, and I even missed out on job opportunities. It wasn't until I reached my early 30's that I realized that my big mouth and nasty attitude blocked a lot of my blessings.

Not only did I have a bad attitude, and a big mouth – I led a very promiscuous lifestyle. My demeanor towards men and the way I dressed did not represent the kingdom, at all! The tighter my clothes, the better. I now know that my lack of self-worth was a big correlation to the way that I carried myself. Again, no one close to me tried to rectify my behavior. They just let me run around looking a hot mess, and of course, talking about me. And to be quite honest, even if they tried to tell me that I needed to change some things about me, I wouldn't have listened anyway. During that phase of my life, you couldn't tell me anything! I knew it all, and I portrayed that in every area of my life.

God surely broke me out of that!

In 2012, God allowed me to relocate from the Bay Area to Georgia. I lived there for approximately ten months. During the duration of my time there, I had several encounters with God. I like to tell people that I met God in Georgia. While I grew up in church, it wasn't until I was more than 3,000 miles away from everything and everyone that I knew that God showed me his character, mercy, love, grace, and favor. 2 Corinthians 6:17 (NLT) says, *Therefore, come out from among unbelievers, and separate yourselves from them, says the Lord. Don't touch their filthy things, and I will welcome you.* In hindsight, I realized that God needed to separate me so that he can begin the process of refining me. the people I called friends weren't focused on serving God, and it was my season to dive deep into my purpose, but I wasn't focused, and I definitely wasn't ready.

In the Bible, the number ten represents obedience and responsibility of people towards God's law. God took me out of my comfort zone to teach me how to be obedient to Him and his word. And let me tell you! That was NOT an easy assignment for me. But I am so very thankful for that assignment. I learned what it means when people say, "There's a blessing in the breaking." God broke me down as if I was a glass vessel. He also began remolding me into a new vessel; a vessel that has no residue of her past. A vessel that can hold the power and presence of God. A vessel that can hold her purpose.

It was there, in Georgia, that God told me that this big mouth of mine would be used to empower women and help restore his daughters. It was there that God told me that my writing would be used to bring glory to his kingdom. It was there that God transformed my mindset and begin molding me into a new version of myself. A version that was unfamiliar to me, and certainly unfamiliar to those who know the Jessica before moving to Georgia.

While I heard God tell me that he would use my writing to bring him glory, I laughed. And then I ran.

I was NOT ready to become a super Christian. I was used to writing naughty poems, ratchet short stories, and raunchy blogs. I wasn't trying to write inspirational, faith-based content. Not even a little bit. I remember the first time I wrote a faith-based poem. I was sitting at my desk at work, and it was as if Holy Spirit took over my pen. After I was done writing, I read it and dropped my pen as I said, "Eugh!"

Yes, I was that far away from God. But still close enough to hear him call my name. It would be years before I give God my complete YES to do His will. I wasn't ready to leave my state of brokenness. I was comfortable being broken. I knew that zone. I didn't know what it meant or felt like to be whole, to be refined and it *scared* me.

Would I have to stop cussing? Drinking? Partying? Having random sex with men that I wasn't in a relationship with? Do I have to start wearing those long dresses to church that won't hug my curves? *Please* don't tell me that I have to stop smoking weed!

I wasn't trying to be on a platform talking about Jesus, God, and the Bible. I'm Jessi B from

Parchester! I'm loud, hood, and ratchet. I like to wear tight clothes and twerk. Sure, I grew up in church, know the Word, served as an usher and even was a Sunday School teacher – but I'm no evangelist. I'm not good enough. Not polished enough. I don't walk around reciting Christian jargon. I don't tell people to have a blessed day, shout hallelujah during service, and I definitely don't attend church every Sunday.

In my mind, I was a weed-smoking, vodka drinking, club-hopping, ratchet dressing chick with no intention of changing my lifestyle.

But God said otherwise.

I Surrender

Once I moved back to California, the seed that God planted in my spirit through another woman of God started to grow. Slowly but surely, I stopped smoking weed, drinking vodka, partying, drifted away from having random men in my bed; I even worked on not cussing as much. I joined a new church, where I learned how to effectively study and apply the Word of God into my life. God was really moving in my life and it was showing. I switched the genre that I wrote and started writing Christian fiction and devotionals.

The one thing that I did not do was change the way that I dressed.

Listen, wearing tight jeans, especially with holes in them, was my *thing*. I wore tight, low-cut shirts showing off every curve God gave me because you couldn't tell me that I wasn't cute. I thought that I was so sexy, and I wanted everyone else to see it, too. Why, though? I would eventually learn why after fully surrendering to God.

One day, I heard God clear as day tell me, "You can't dress like that anymore. I can't position you in front of my daughters looking like the world." I agreed to change my wardrobe. And I had every intention to, especially after seeing the plans God had for my life. The vision that God showed me excited me. I wanted to become this woman. I definitely knew it would be a process to become her and I was willing to go *and* grow through the process.

Well, I guess I wasn't moving fast enough for God and he forced me to change my wardrobe on his terms.

One particular weekend, I decided to wash all of my clothes at the laundromat. At that time, I'd normally only wash two loads: a colored load and a white load. This weekend, I felt led to wash all of my clothes. I did my usual routine of dropping my clothes off at the laundromat, going to the Dollar Tree, coming back to switch my clothes from the washer to the dryer, going to the grocery store or Walmart, and then coming back to get my dried clothes.

My routine started just fine. I went to check on my clothes before going to Walmart, and my white load was dried, so I put them in the car. I still had about 45 minutes for my colored load, so I went to Walmart. As I'm strolling through the aisle, I get this feeling in my gut that tells me – I've been in this store too long. When I get back to the laundromat, I noticed that not only are my baskets missing but so are my clothes! All three loads that I had drying were gone!

I was livid! The owner of the facility was of no help and I was devastated! What was I going to wear? I had nothing….

I remember calling my mom, crying, feeling so defeated, telling her someone stole my clothes. I was mad because the money I'd been saving over the prior weeks would have to be used for me to go shopping, rather than having a little something for a rainy day. Under different circumstances, having to shop for a new wardrobe would have been the highlight of my day. But that wasn't the case and I wasn't happy. At all.

As I sat on my bed, thinking about my favorite outfits that I'd never see again, and staring at my bare closet, God said, "I told you to get rid of those clothes." And all I could do was laugh. Yep, I laughed! I couldn't even be mad anymore. I was being hardheaded, and God had to show me that he wasn't playing with me. He said, what He said.

It was then that I realized the assignment that God gave me was bigger than me and some stupid clothes. And that *really* scared me. Although God reassured me that I'd be in the palm of his unchanging hand, that he'd lead me towards the right path, and be with me every step of the way - I still didn't feel worthy enough of being a part of something so impactful. In my mind, I wasn't good enough to give God glory on a public platform. And to be completely honest, I was still broken.

I was still angry that my daughter's father didn't consistently support my daughter. I was angry that the people I called my friend betrayed me. I was hurt that my family members didn't support my dream to be an author. I was ashamed of my past. And I just couldn't see why God would want me to encourage other women in any way, shape, or form.

Nope, I can't do this God stuff. It's too much....

Besides, if I can be completely transparent: it was easier for me to be broken, then healed. But that wasn't what God wanted for me. And I'm so glad that He changed my mind.

Process of Refinement

While I thought I was running away from being refined, God had already started the process, which is why I was in so much pain. Not only did God remove my old wardrobe, he started to remove my closest friends. When I asked God why he said that I couldn't remain friends with people who would keep me bound.

While I understood the logic, I was a little upset. Who was I supposed to talk to now? Hang out with? Bounce ideas off of? God showed me that I didn't need anyone but Him during that season of my life.

When God wants to refine you, He will separate you so He can heal you without distractions. The people closest to us are our biggest distraction. Because these people embrace our old way of thinking, behaving, and reacting, they tend to disrupt our season of refinement. Know that when God is refining you, it will be a lonely journey.

Now, be aware; there are three steps to refinement. Although there are three steps, it's going to take a long time to complete these steps. So don't set yourself up for disappointment and think this is something that will happen overnight because it won't. And the steps are so potent, that you don't want them to happen too quickly. You want to be able to absorb the wisdom, knowledge, and understanding that you'll gain while being refined. So, what are the three steps?

Step One: Isolation. The first thing God will do is isolate you. He removes you from your comfort zone because He is developing your mindset, polishing your spirit, and perfecting your heart. He can't afford for you to be confused or misled. So he has to take you away from people and environments that will deter you from following through with the process.

Step Two: Pruning. The second thing God will do is prune you. During this step, He's removing unnecessary traits, thoughts, and sentiments that will no longer serve you. He replaces them with traits, thoughts, and sentiments of more substance. Before God can position you in the kingdom, He has to prune you. He's not going to set you up to fail, so therefore, He has to equip you with the right mindset so you can make the right decisions that will lead to your purpose.

Step Three: Molding. The third thing God will do is mold you. Once He gets you away from people who will contaminate your thoughts, removes negative traits, and perverse sentiments from your spirit, He then begins to shape you into the woman He created you to be. God literally will reconstruct your mind, heart, and spirit. He will take the broken parts of you and turn them into a foundation that will hold the new version of you.

These three steps may seem like you can handle the process, but let me tell you, sis: being refined HURTS! It doesn't feel good to be alone, it's not fun when God removes your familiar traits and it's certainly not fun being rebuilt into a different version of yourself. Like I mentioned earlier, it's easy to stay broken, it's familiar. But when God starts to show you visions and dreams of the life that He wants you to have and you feel unworthy, you'll sabotage His plans and will forfeit the promise on your life. This is why you have to be refined before you can be positioned.

Trust me, I understand why you would run away from God. I mean, who in their right minds would agree to being refined? No one! You already know that it's going to hurt, so why volunteer to be subjected to pain?

Well, pain leads to purpose.

As the saying goes: no pain, no gain. And it's true. When you are truly seeking the Kingdom of God in hopes to have everything you desire added to your life, know that the road won't be fun or easy at times. Kingdom Business is serious and it's not for the faint of heart. Sure, you'll want to quit during the process, but how will you ever see the promised land if you don't keep walking?

Understand that God needs you to trust that He knows what He's doing. No, the refinement process isn't easy. But nothing worth

having ever is. Be still and know that He is…
Because, well… He is…

Becoming A Resilient Queen

When God showed me the vision of me speaking on stages and coaching women, I felt unworthy yet excited. I can't believe I'm starting to live out that vision. And no, it's not something that happened overnight. It happened day by day, week by week, month by month, year by year, choice by choice, mistake after mistake, failure after failure, heartache after heartache.

But it happened to me. And know that it will happen for you.

The moment you decide that you're tired of running from God and you're finally ready to submit, that's when you'll see growth, evolution, and experience true healing. Before God can give you the desires of your heart, He has to remove the impurities and unwanted elements from your life. Yes! It's all a process. There is no new season, or new you without going through a process. And that process ain't pretty and it ain't fun. But that's where you gain some of the best qualities as a daughter of the Most High.

During the process of being refined, I learned what it meant to be classy, Christ-like, and resilient. I experienced so many setbacks while shifting from the old version of me, but they were truly lessons to equip me for the next level God is taking me. It was unfamiliar territory and it made me uncomfortable, but it's been oh so worth it. The wisdom, knowledge, discernment, and patience I've gained over the years doesn't compare to anything I've ever experienced.

Everyone's process of refinement will look different but will be just as powerful and transformational. Becoming a resilient queen takes time, dedication and faith. If you truly want to become a better you, you have to be willing to trust God and do the work.

So, what would I say to another woman who grew up with an attitude, smart mouth, and sassy ways, but desire to become happy, healed and whole? Well, there are three things you should do:

1. **Be honest about your state of brokenness.** For *years* I would lie to myself and say that I didn't care about being single, or that I wasn't hurt when I ended my friendship with my best friend, or that it didn't bother

me that my daughter's father didn't help me, but I did care, I was hurt, and it did bother me. When I admitted how I truly felt, it made it easier to address my pain and release it.

2. **Know that it's okay to be by yourself for a season or two.** We get so caught up in always being surrounded by people that we don't know how to function when we're alone. In Ecclesiastes 3, the Word of God says there's a time for everything – and that includes being alone. You don't always have to have friends or a man in your life. It's okay to take some time to learn yourself and bond with God. I recommend that you do.

3. **Understand your healing and your help will only come from God.** Not people, not alcohol, not the club, not sex, not a drug but Almighty God himself. When you realize that your journey is a one-woman show, it becomes easier to release people and things that don't bring out the best in you. It becomes easier releasing the wrong people, ending the wrong circumstances, and walking away from toxic environments. There isn't anything or anyone on this earth that has power over

your life. God has been and will always be your source for all good things.

I know that becoming a resilient queen isn't comfortable, but the process is necessary. I truly believe that I am apart of God's royal priesthood and that I'm royalty. I honestly believe that I'm worthy of every good thing God has me. I know that I have a place in God's kingdom, despite my dirty past, and that brings me joy. I pray that you become confident in who *you* are and learn *your* place in the kingdom and boldly show up as her.

I am so grateful for all of the disappointments, let downs, frustrating situations, betrayal, closed doors, and rock bottom moments I've faced. It was during the times when people talked about me, left me hanging, or didn't support me that I learned just who I am in Christ. I learned not to let my past define me. I learned not to be bothered by the naysayers. I saw first-hand that God will prepare a table in the presence of my enemies if I keep my eyes focused on Him.

Being a queen isn't about being arrogant, bragging or boasting. It's about tapping into your purpose, seeking the kingdom first, and allowing God to give you the desires of your heart, on his terms.

As you are allowing God to mold you into a new vessel and embracing your inner queen, know that you deserve every opportunity and abundant experience that God will bless you with. Don't feel bad for growing, healing, and evolving. Don't allow your past to prevent you from leading a life of purpose. The word of God says that when we are in Christ, we are new creatures. That means that you have the right to act brand new because you are.

Know that God loves you and that when God looks at you, He sees beauty, power, purpose, and resilience. You are amazing, you are important, and we need your essence on this earth. So my sister-queen-girlfriend, allow God to build your throne, give you a new crown, and rock it like the queen that you are. You're worthy...

Be Ye Restored

Written by Angela Robertson

And a woman was there who had been subject to bleeding for twelve years, but no one could heal her. She came up behind him and touched the edge of his cloak, and immediately her bleeding stopped.

Luke 8:43-44

Before I hit rock bottom in my life, I knew I wanted to have a good life and be successful, but I felt lost. I was living my life based on reacting to whatever happened to me instead of purposefully designing my life. My thinking pattern was street mentality, hustle hard, and figure it out as I go. I learned the street mentality while living at my mom's house. Growing up in Oakland helped me survive the environment I was in, but I knew there was more to life than struggle, poverty, and dysfunction. As a child, I was exposed to a different way of living when my mom sent me away to live with my godmother. My godmother was truly a godmother. She was heavily involved in church and worked as a beautician. She lived in Suisun, CA and she worked and attended church in Oakland, CA. The church we attended was Evergreen Missionary Baptist Church. Mrs. James took very good care of me. I had my room designed like an antique dollhouse, we took trips out of town and ate at different restaurants. I did not understand at the time, however, why we had to go to church so much. Mrs. James was a part of the choir, Pastor's Aide Committee, we went to Bible study every week and fellowship every Sunday- not to mention the special events at church. Besides going to church, Mrs. James kept my hair whipped. She put me in pageants where I learned princess etiquette and how to build my self-esteem. I remember one pageant I won almost every category except for the title. I felt like I should have won the title as well. Hindsight, I now see what I was missing. It was revealed to me after I hit rock bottom later on in my life. My godmother would take me with her to her friends' houses who lived in the Oakland Hills in what I considered to be mansions. I lived with Mrs. James from age 8 to 11/12 years old. I was baptized at the age of 10 believing that God can help me live a prosperous life. The spirit of God was at work in my life, but I did not make the associations until later on in life. I started to excel rapidly in school and was ahead of my class. Since I was excelling in school, the school told my godmother that I was ready to skip a grade.

When I called my mom to tell her great news, she sent for me to come back home. I did miss my mom and brothers, but I had no idea that the shift in life I was headed towards was going to bring me to my biggest downfall. There was a big difference in environments and the mentality of my mom's house and my godmother's house. At my mom's house, no one went to church and we lived in the projects on Section 8. When I noticed that my room walls were full of mildew in the winter; that my mom was rarely home; and how I had to clean up after my brothers, so I would not get in trouble, I begged my godmother to live back with her again. My Godmother allowed me to live with her again for a few months, but her health was rapidly declining and she "no longer could keep up with me" as she told my mom. I felt rejected and I was depressed that I had to come back to my mom's house.

Good thing I received Jesus Christ as my personal Lord and Savior at the age of 10 while living with my godmother because I was going to need it. The environment at my mom's house had gotten worse with men that were gang bangers, drug dealers, and pimps running in and out of the house- all of whom are now either dead or in jail far as I know. Often my mom would take me to the free food place to volunteer and receive free food when we ran out around the end of the month. By the age of 14, I was kicked out of school for fighting, not attending church and being raised by thugs, drug dealers, and pimps. By the age of 15, I was in a relationship with my now ex-husband, an illegal entrepreneur and plotting on how to get out of the hood. Although I did not go to church every Sunday, there were times I would pop into Grace Temple Missionary Baptist Church. At one point I attended regularly because I knew I needed help.

By the age of 18, I saved up enough money to move out of my mom's house and I moved to Richmond with my ex-husband. Even though I knew in my heart he was not for me, I allowed the fact that we've been together for five years at the time dictate the rest of my life. I broke up with him many times, but I had this thing about me that wanted to remain loyal to those who were loyal to me especially during that difficult time in my life. I learned that loyalty is a good quality to have but be careful who you become loyal to. I was tired of the feeling of being used and I wanted out! I was tired of the mental abuse and I wanted out! I was tired of being intimidated and talked down to and I wanted out! I was tired of being ignored for weeks at a time and I wanted out! I was tired of rarely ever being told thank you, I appreciate you, you're beautiful, you're cute, or even you look good and I wanted out!

But then I found out that I was pregnant.

So, I am now in an unhealthy relationship, pregnant and spiritually lost. Do I abort the baby and move on with my life? No, I was forced to do that once and I vowed that I'll never do that again. That's a whole 'nother story. I've had a miscarriage as well and I still remember the pain of thinking that I was going to start my own family, but it was snatched away. The period of depression I went through made me want a baby even more. I've always wanted a family and he seemed to be happy that I was pregnant. He promised to change so I changed my mind and stayed with him. It wasn't long before the "honeymoon stage" was over, the smoke cleared and I realized that he was not going to change, in fact, our relationship got worse.

I learned the hard way that a baby does not make a bad relationship better, it makes it more complicated. After I had the baby, a friend invited me to church. After I attended, I knew that this was not the life God wanted me to live. Long story short, I left, and I should have never looked back.

Unfortunately, I did look back.

About a year later after I moved out and set up visitation for him and our daughter, which was a waste of time. Why? Because I was back in bed with him and within a month, I got pregnant again. Now we are about to have another baby - daughter number two, and I am in conflict with myself once again. I overlooked all the problems and I figure it would be the right thing to do to keep our family together. I wanted to believe that this time he was going to change. We agreed that marriage would be the best thing for our growing family. Even though family members and friends questioned me about marrying him, I canceled them out and focused on what I thought was the right thing to do. We declined marriage counseling and within months we were married.

Instead of consulting with God first, on my wedding day it hit me, I am about to make a promise to God to stay with this man for life. At that moment I asked God for a sign to show me if he did not want me to go through with this. That was silly, right? Why would I wait until my wedding day to talk to God about a decision I had already made. Hindsight, maybe the fact that my mom's refusal to show up was my sign that marrying him was a bad decision. Maybe the almost fatal car accident that happened right after the wedding on our way to our honeymoon in

Reno was a sign that marrying him was a bad decision. But for the sake of my family, I decided to ride it out. Although we had good times, the bad outweighed the good but I still decided to ride it out. I was the definition of a ridah. I soon realized that marriage does not change people. In fact, more of who you are comes out in marriage. I was following a man who did not follow God and it felt like I was just being used and manipulated. I felt like my presence irritated him because he seemed to be mad often but could not explain why. Communication was often one-sided while I was left to figure out his next move. My money was our money, and his money was his money. Secret trips and random "emergencies" took him away from the house at odd hours and the focus became only about the girls when he was home. Yes, I wanted my family together, but I also wanted to be loved, appreciated and treated with care. It felt like the only attention I received was when he wanted something.

The Evangelistic Encounter

One day while networking in the community I came across a man who was with his two boys. I delivered my spill to recruit his sons to a modeling agency that I was marketing for. I also introduced their dad to another business I was growing at the time. Although I was married, I felt like most of the financial responsibility fell on my shoulders. Now having a family, I stopped doing illegal side businesses and hustled legally while working whatever job I could find. Later I started a home childcare business and let go of all those side businesses. The man agreed to take a look at my side business with his wife and invited me to church. I originally thought his church would be a good place for me to network for business but when I attended his church the following Sunday, I received a life-changing word. I prayed for God to guide me. One night, I noticed my ex-husband's phone was on silent with random messages coming through that he refused to answer. Long story short, I called and talked to this mystery person and found out he had been cheating on me. Fury raged in me and I lost my mind! I was done trying to build a family with somebody who continuously took my kindness for weakness. Who continuously did what was best for him not what was best for our family.

Through his begging for me not to leave him he said, "But we never tried marriage counseling." Life for him was comfortable, why would he want to mess that up? But he was right, and I gave in, vowing this was the last time! I wanted to make peace that I did all that I could do. I showed up to church the next Sunday and so did he, asking for marriage counseling. For some reason I still had hope. I felt stupid, confused and lost on what to do. I didn't want to be another single Black mother, but I was also done with allowing this man to treat me this way. Insecurities came over me and I started to question if something was wrong with me. Am I not pretty enough, am I not smart enough, am I too tall, is it my flabby baby stomach, and the list went on and on. These insecurities stuck with me as I continued to cater to a man that did not deserve me. I felt stuck but I felt a sense of hope being covered by a man of God and going through marriage counseling.

The Pastor at Rock Harbor Christian fellowship counseled us. Every time we went to counseling, I felt like there was hope. Often within hours after counseling, the atmosphere in our home changed right back to anger and manipulation. I found out through counseling that the anger issues he was dealing with stemmed from his childhood and that was something I could not help with. It seemed to me that no matter what I did, I could not make him happy. Without notice, he would leave for hours, returning without any interaction with me or truth about where he had been. I felt helpless and angry and I didn't know what to do.

The mental abuse caused me to continue to question what was wrong with me. As I continued to attend church, the wedge between us became more obvious. I have learned that in relationships, either you are growing together, or you are growing apart. I believe this is what is meant when the Bible says in 2 Corinthians 6:14 (NLV), "Don't team up with those who are unbelievers. How can righteousness be a partner with wickedness? How can light live with darkness?" I wanted to live my life in right standing with God and take care of my family in peace. But there was no peace in the home. Hindsight, I realize it was the enemy working through him disturbing our peace and destroying our family.

We continued through marriage counseling until I caught him cheating again. I didn't look for it nor did I want to believe it when the situation slapped me in the face. I knew that this is not what God wanted for me. The mind games no longer worked on me and all I wanted was for him to get out of my house. When he saw that he could no longer control me, he flipped out. When I refused to allow him to sleep in the bed with me, he flipped the bed over and somehow a board swapped me across my face and busted my ear. The room was dark, and he will not admit to hitting me with the board but all I know is that my ear was busted. And I'll be honest, I tried to break his jaw! I'm not perfect, I fight back!!

My Pastor and the man that introduced me to the church escorted him out of the house. I praise God for deliverance, but I was deeply hurt. I still had to interact with him because of the girls but I see why women take their children and run. The weird part is he still thought he could get me to have sex with him. Maybe because I gave in before, but I was serious this time and he couldn't believe it. I felt angry and fearful when he tried to force himself on me. No longer would I do what he told me to do- especially have sex with him. The infidelity, mental, then physical, then sexual abuse was the last sign I needed to know that marrying him was a bad decision. Months later he asked for a divorce.

The Road to Freedom

Although I was relieved to be delivered from that bondage, rejection still hit me like a thief in the night. What I wanted was for him to change. I was hoping that I was enough for him to change, him keeping his family together was enough for him to change, or at least knowing how much he was hurting me was enough for him to change but it wasn't. I was hoping that God could change him, but I realize that even God cannot change someone who does not want to be changed. I felt used, manipulated, and hopeless. My heart was broken, and I resented him.

Court-ordered visitation for the children was set up to minimize as much confusion and fights as possible. At first, every phone conversation turned into more manipulation and name-calling when my ex couldn't get what he wanted. Phone conversations ceased and all communications went through text messages to minimize arguments and the "he said she said." At first, my ex could come to pick up the children from home but after fighting him off of me a few times from sexual attacks, pickups went curbside. After a couple of verbal outbursts and threats from the curb, the pickups went to the Bart station and a restraining order was put in place.

After the restraining order lifted, sexual attacks at the Bart station reconvened and threats thereafter when I would not comply. And for the first time, I called the police instead of my pastor or my ex's dad, but I did not press charges. I could not stand the thought of my daughters not being able to see their dad or them knowing why their dad was in jail. As foolish as it sounds, I was still trying to protect their relationship. Another restraining order was put in place and pick up arrangements for the children changed to pickups at the children's school. On the days of no school, pickups and drop-offs were set near a police station to minimize and govern interactions.

When my ex could not have his way with me anymore, threats came at me like fiery darts. Anxiety attacks were like a plague and I started to frantically run around looking to see how I could fill this void and relieve the pain. Restraining orders did not help relieve the fear. Mental health therapy groups didn't help with the anger and depression that I felt. Smoking weed made me feel better in the moment, but things seemed to get worse after the high went down. Had I known the Word of God at the time I could have been comforted by this scripture, Psalm 118:5-7 (NIV) "When hard pressed, I cried to the Lord; he brought me into a spacious place. The

Lord is with me; I will not be afraid. What can mere mortals do to me? The Lord is with me; he is my helper. I look in triumph on my enemies." I could have spoken Philippians 4:7 (NIV) over my life, "And the peace of God, which transcends all understanding, will guard your hearts and your minds in Christ Jesus."

I also had a fear of the unknown moving forward, fear of being alone, fear of falling into poverty and fear of death. But I remembered a song we used to sing in the choir with my godmother that said, "God hath not given us the spirit of fear, but the Lord hath given us power! Power and love, his joy and peace, his happiness, He hath given us a sound mind. Never shall I be afraid!" I later learned that that song came from the word of God - 2 Timothy 1:7.

I was not mad at God for not fixing my marriage, but I did feel ashamed to approach God with my mess of a life. One thing I did know from going to church is that God is a forgiver and we must forgive others if we want God to forgive us. But I did not want to forgive him.

As my anxiety decreased, my anger increased. I was angry and I felt justified to act a fool. I wanted to put God on the shelf for a moment and handle him myself. That hood mentality started to rise in me, and I thought about every man that I knew who would have laid him down for me. I kept what I was going through with my ex a secret from my family because I knew he would get hurt.

When my mom came over to spend time with the girls, she found out some of the stuff that was happening, and she flashed. The advice I received from her caused anxiety to rise in me again. I knew that if I did what she was telling me to do, it was going to be an all-out war, and somebody was going to die. I thought about my daughters and how I grew up without a dad. I thought that it was the right thing to do by making sure my daughters had their dad in their life. I knew I had to fight for my peace, but I wanted to do it the right way. I choose to believe that God had something better for me and I wasn't going to allow the enemy to continue to destroy my life.

The Gift of Salvation

Finally, I chose to run to God. God has always been there, but I had to see that I was full of sin and it was not just my ex. I chose to have sex with him outside of a covenant and that was wrong. I chose to put people and things before God and that was wrong. I chose to marry him without consulting with God and that was wrong. There were many things that I did that was against God's Will. I was beating myself up for what I did to my life and I wanted to die. 1 John 1:8-9 says "If we say we have no sin, we deceive ourselves, and the truth is not in us. If we confess our sins, He is faithful and just to forgive us our sins and to cleanse us from all unrighteousness" I had to find a way to humble myself and ask God for forgiveness and believe in his Word that he will cleanse me from all unrighteousness. At this moment John 3:16-17 came to life. "For God so loved the world that he gave his one and only Son, that whoever believes in him shall not perish but have eternal life. For God did not send his Son into the world to condemn the world, but to save the world through him." God gave me the gift of salvation. I had a choice: to accept God's gift, or not. I chose to accept God's gift of salvation believing that God can help me build a better life. The Word of God also says in Colossians 3:13 "Bear with each other and forgive one another if any of you has a grievance against someone. Forgive as the Lord forgave you." It took a minute but I chose to forgive him and others so I could receive forgiveness from

God. I had to learn how to accept an apology from him, and other people, that they never gave me; and forgive them even though I did not want to. Unforgiveness is like being in prison in the mind and allowing your emotions to control you. Unforgiveness is like being a slave to the person who harmed you and allowing what they did to control you. I had to take control of my emotions and thoughts by having self-control, not reacting to what he does, and ignoring the negativity. Forgiveness does not mean I had to be around him. Forgiveness allows healing to flow. You see, hurt people, hurt people, and I have decided that the hurt stops with me. I decided to forgive him. I've learned that even though I am required to forgive him, I do not have to give him my time. As the Word of God says, "Submit yourselves, then, to God. Resist the devil, and he will flee from you." James 4:7 (NIV)

Everything I was worried about, God had already promised to take care of it if I just believed in Him. From going to church, I remember a scripture that says, "But seek ye first the kingdom of God, and his righteousness; and all these things shall be added unto you." Matthew 6:33 (KJV). Later on, I found out what that meant. In Matthew 6:30-33 (MSG) the Bible states, "If God gives such attention to the appearance of wildflowers—most of which are never even seen—don't you think he'll attend to you, take pride in you, do his best for you? What I'm trying to do here is to get you to relax, to not be so preoccupied with getting, so you can respond to God's giving. People who don't know God and the way he works fuss over these things, but you know both God and how he works. Step into God's-reality, God's-initiative, and God's-provisions. Don't worry about missing out. You'll find all your everyday human concerns will be met." I can rejoice in that! I shout hallelujah, giving God the highest praise. The challenge was figuring out how to receive the blessing. Do I just pray and wait for money to magically appear? I wanted to believe that God was going to take care of me, but I also know from the scriptures that faith without works is dead. Meaning that it's good to believe but I also have to do something for God to guide me. My prayer became "Lord open the doors you have for me and close the ones that are not for me. I declare all my needs are met according to Your Word."

I remembered what my mom did when we did not have enough so I started there. I sought out free food places, shopped more at the dollar store, applied for welfare, and looked for housing assistance programs. As I stood in lines and waited for my number to be called, I thought to myself, *I do not belong here, this is not the life God has for me.* I never liked the feeling of asking for a handout, but I needed help. I used the programs for a leg up not a continuous hand out. I declared that my past will not equal the future.

I love my mom, but I did not want to end up like her. I watched how she masked her pain with being tough and drowned her sorrows in weed and alcohol. I watched how she scraped pennies together each month to get by but always seemed to have advice on what everybody else needed to do for success. I remember telling her about how I was struggling, and her best advice was that I better learn how to turn some tricks. The hood loved my mom because she always kept it "real". What's happening in the times we live in doesn't mean that it is right. I just so happen to be in pursuit of righteousness, and I dismissed that advice with disgust as soon as it was delivered. I'm so glad I did not buy her opinion of what I should have done because I would have bought her lifestyle as well. I thank God for the opportunity I had with my mom to allow forgiveness and healing to flow between us before she passed away in February 2014. I also thank God that she accepted Jesus Christ as her

Lord and Savior and was baptized before she passed away. It's too bad she did not get to witness my current marriage because she truly adored Trevor, my current husband. Rest in perfect peace, mom.

Failing Forward

During that time, however, I did not have anyone I could turn to for help. I remember visiting with family members and friends who could not help me. Some listened and told me it would be okay, and some thought that I had gone crazy for sure. I tried to shake it off by fixing myself up and going out on weekends while my girls were at their dad's house for his time with them. Every time I went out, I felt awkward and out of place. I remember a man at a club told me, "You do not belong here." As I looked at other women in the club, I thought maybe he said that because I needed to be a little sexier. Maybe it was something too proper about how I stood and/or sat at the bar. I found a way to loosen up and have fun after a few drinks. After a few drinks, I would have a few dances. At the end of it all, I just wanted to go home. I didn't want a hookup nor was I looking for a man. But men were looking for me. As I saw men looking and lurking to see who they can devour, I realized why clubs are not my scene.

One day a friend/business associate of mine invited me on a road trip to Las Vegas to see the Mayweather fight. I told her I did not want to go after she told me who was going. She said it was going to be her, her male friend, her cousin and her cousin's husband. It sounded like I was going to be the fifth wheel, so I did not want to go. She reassured me that her male friend was just a friend, that she was married and had other friends that we were going to meet when we got to Las Vegas as well. She told me that she will pay for my hotel stay and gas if we could use my van for the ride. I agreed to go and was excited to get out of the house. She told me she needed me to pick up her male friend from his house on the way to her house and that was the first time I met Trevor.

We chatted on the way to her house, chatted on the way to Vegas, chatted while in Vegas, and barely said anything to each other on the way back from Vegas. Our eyes said it all. We found out that were in similar situations dealing with lying, cheating, manipulative ex's and currently separated. I was newly separated, and Trevor had been separated for 6 years. On the drive back from Vegas I saw him constantly looking back at me from the passenger seat. I knew he was feeling me, and I was feeling him, too. After we dropped everybody off to their destinations and we were alone, I asked him, "Why you kept looking at me in the car?" he answered, "Because I'm feeling you." I replied, "I'm feeling you, too." We dated for a little over a month, he treated me like a Queen, but he kept saying he is not ready for a relationship. I was confused because we were doing all the relationship type stuff, but he wanted to stay "friends". Since I saw that he had other female friends I started to question his relationship with them. I was back in conflict. All my free time and energy was being put into him. I realized that I liked this man too much and we were moving too fast and going nowhere. Truth be told, I was not ready for an intimate relationship either and I was out of the Will of God once again, so I left him. I left him and I did not think twice about it.

I cut off all communication and focused on my children and childcare business that was dying slowly. Even though I was still attending church, I was still looking for something to fill this void I had in my life. While at a friend's house one day, I ran into an old friend. A familiar face that I had not seen in a very long time. He was my friend's cousin and my second boyfriend when I was about 12 or 13. After catching up on life I found out he had been through a lot and was currently in a rough situation with his daughter. His daughter was given to him by the courts because her mom was fighting a murder case. He had to go back and forth to court with her and needed help. Before I knew it, he and his daughter were in my home while I sought how to help him. Since he had to leave Sacramento and come to Oakland for his daughter, he had to find a new job, living arrangements and schooling for his daughter until the courts made a decision. It was the middle of summer and my girls were with their dad for his half and I was extremely lonely and depressed. Before I knew it, things between me and the old friend started to rekindle as we drowned our pain in alcohol and weed.

What I once put down, I picked back up again. This time, it was worse. I wanted to stop but the weed seemed to numb my pain and the alcohol seemed to release it. When the high came down, I felt even worse which prompted me to use again. And again. Until it was time for my daughters to come home. Everything had to go! Including him. But he did not want to go. In fact, he told me he was not leaving. All the attempts to find him a job and a place to live failed and he felt I was his only hope. But I did not want my girls to come home to a stranger and it was never the plan for him to live there.

Unfortunately, he refused to leave. Matter of fact, when I moved, he moved. Just like that. When it was time to pick up the girls from their dad, there he was sitting in the passenger seat mean mugging my ex. When it was time to go to Bible study that Wednesday, he did his best to convince me not to go. But I went anyway and so did he. He became like a leech in my life. I expressed to my Pastor what was going on and how I needed him to leave. After my Pastor spoke with him, he assured me that he was going to find somewhere else to stay. But when we got back to my house the whole story changed to how he is not leaving. He demanded me to help him like I said I was. I did not want to call the police and cause a scene and put more drama inside of his daughter's life or my life. He could not see that I could barely help myself. I lost weight faster than I ever imagined and I looked sick. I *was* sick. I talked to his family members and they told me they are willing to help him, so I felt relieved and we planned for him to leave.

The same week, the girls started school, I started taking college courses to obtain my Early Childhood Education Degree from Contra Costa College. I was working out childcare for my daughters, but the old friend convinced me to let my daughters stay with him for those few hours while I went to school since his daughter and niece were there as well. My daughters seemed comfortable to stay as they played with the other girls. My only rule was that if they did something wrong, do not put his hands on them. Do not whoop them. He agreed.

When I got back home from school, I was told that the girls got in trouble, but they did not get a whooping. I sent them to bed early as a punishment. The next day the girls went back with their dad for the weekend. Next thing I know, CPS was at my front door saying that a report has been filed saying my girls were being abused. The report said that a man tied their hands up and put them in the closet. I was furious! I asked the old friend what happened, and he kept repeating, "I did not put my hands on them kids!" My ex felt like he had something to attack me with and he used it to his advantage. Death threats were more like promises. I talked to my girls when they got back home but I was so upset that they could not see how this was blown out of proportion. But I apologized to them because what if they did get hurt? I regretted leaving my daughters with him because I thought my ex was about to kill me. I had to realize that the fear I felt was false evidence appearing real. If I sent my daughters to school and something happened to them while they are at school, was my ex going to kill me for sending them to school or attack the wrongdoer? If I sent the girls to his house and something happened to the girls while they are at his house, is he going to kill me for sending them to his house or attack the wrongdoer? I am not the wrongdoer in this equation so I should not be attacked. The truth of the matter is he was looking for something to attack me because I no longer would do what he wanted me to do.

On the other hand, the old friend is now in my ear saying the reason he does not want to leave is because he loves me and wants to marry me. I felt like I was in a twilight zone. Panic attacks were hitting hard until one night I grabbed my girls and fled to my Pastor's house. I told him I was not going to leave until that man is out of my house. The next day, the man who introduced me to the church and Pastor Port escorted the old friend out of my house and was told not to come back. He apologized and left. I was in a worse state of mind and spiritual position than I was when me and my ex and I initially separated. There was not a shadow of doubt that I needed God desperately.

Kingdom Business

One Sunday as I sat in the congregation, I felt like the Pastor was talking to me throughout his sermon. He said, there is no condemnation for those who are in Christ Jesus. I remember thinking "then I must not be in Christ because I still feel condemned and ashamed." I was ashamed that I put my relationship with my ex and other people before God. I was ashamed of allowing dysfunction for the sake of keeping my family together. I was feeling condemned because I knew God hates divorce and I felt like a failure. I felt ashamed that my children would have to see the dysfunction and experience a broken family. I felt ashamed of using weed and alcohol to numb my pain. I felt guilty for allowing that man in my home and not being there to protect my daughters. I was broke financially, relationally and spiritually. The guilt of what I had done to my life and my children's life made me feel like I wanted to die. Thoughts of suicide entered my mind, but my children became my reason to live. I had to live until God called me home. The sad part is that I even prayed that God would just take my life while I slept. I found myself weeping before the Lord for days. I had, at last, hit rock bottom.

I was searching for peace, love, prosperity, and purpose but I did not know what I was doing. I did know that I had to seek the Kingdom of God, but I still did not know what that meant. I thought it meant to just keep showing up to church, so I did.

At a Bible study on Wednesday night, the Pastor said, "My sheep hear my voice, and I know them, and they follow me." That night at home, I felt a spirit come over me and I prayed, and I rededicated my life back to God. I was trying to express to my Pastor and First Lady how I wanted to be baptized again but they did not think I needed that. I felt I did so I got rebaptized at another church on Easter Sunday in 2011 at Covenant Baptist Church in Berkeley, CA. The following Sunday I remember the Pastor saying cast your cares upon the Lord for He cares about you. I felt so unworthy of God's blessing for my life, but I was desperate. At the time I owned a childcare and I was down to only one child enrolled. I did not receive child support and I did not know what I was going to do financially. I was two months away from receiving an eviction notice. So, I cast my financial care on God. I understood the word when it talked about tithing, so I became obedient in my tithes even though I didn't have enough to pay my rent. I realized that's exactly why I had to pay tithes, I had to show God I trust him with everything. I found a program that helped me with one-month worth of rent through the Bay Area Rescue Mission in Richmond, CA. That gave me hope and I continued to trust God. I continued to tithe and within a couple of months, I had a full childcare with a waiting list to follow. I realized that when I sought after God with my heart, I built a relationship with God through the Word of God. My thinking was transformed, and revelation came forth.

God gave us a very powerful Will. The human Will is so powerful that even God himself cannot override it. I've learned that we have to submit our will to God for Him to work in it. We have to give it to him freely and willingly. We then have to be obedient in the process by giving our yes to God even if we don't know what to do or how to do it. I found out that when I didn't know what to do or how to do it, that's where God does his best work!

I wanted so desperately for His Will to be done in my life and to receive the blessings He promised me through his Word. I ran to God and He became my refuge and strength from that point moving forward. As I built a relationship with God, I built healthy relationships with people. Through the Word of God I found out that God not only supplies our needs, but he also gives us the desires of your hearts. Take a look at Psalm 37:4 NLT "Take delight in the LORD, and he will give you your heart's desires."

Be ye restored is my way of saying that a new life is waiting for you, but you cannot receive it until you put Him first in your life and allow Him to help you out that pit. It doesn't matter how you got in the pit, whether you put yourself in that pit or somebody threw you in the pit. However, it is worth noting that negativity will lead to self-pity which will cause you to live in the pit. Positivity will lead to positive self-esteem which will cause you to live an elevated life. God is the source of positive vibes only. It's time to level up, sis! It's time to experience heaven on earth! It's time to go from the pit to the palace.

We do not deserve God's mercy and grace, but God knew what we were going to go through and that's exactly why He sent Jesus, God in the flesh, to die for our sins. Jesus took the sting away from death so that we may be able to experience a full life. As my Bishop Christopher C. Smith puts it, "A Zoey kind of life. Zoey in the Greek means a heavenly life, a God kind of life. Zoey is the highest quality of life God has to offer mankind."

Now that I am healed, my life is different. Although I am walking out a new life with Christ, the enemy still attacks but my posture is different. As I see God's promises manifest in my life I declare not to ever look back. The more my life becomes peaceful and prosperous, the more my love for God grows. I now do the things my godmother did and more. I now know that it was because of the love of God that my godmother served in the Kingdom as much as she did.

One day, my cousin Rene invited me to a Women's event at her first lady's house. It was at that event a prophetess told me I was going to get remarried and preach the word of God. Although that lady did not know me or my story, she was right. I am now remarried to my best friend and lover, Trevor.

All I know is that since my standards changed, so did he. I was so deep in my relationship with God that he had to go through God to have a relationship with me. I was not willing to be friends with benefits. I was made to be a wife and I wasn't willing to accept anything less. He submitted to God and I submitted to him. That sounds good but in reality, my walk with God is separate from his walk with God. I can easily submit to my husband because I see him submit to God. Again, that sounds good but

I'm not perfect, sometimes I don't want to submit. God is still working on me. I know my husband has my best interest at heart and he treats me like a Queen. Our life has been prosperous and peaceful even more so after we got married. His relationship with the girls is amazing considering he is not their biological father, but he treats them with love and care.

I needed that time by myself before God allowed us back into each other's lives, so God could work on me and build me up into the woman I needed to be for him. Trevor reported that if I did not have high standards, it would not have encouraged him to be the man he is today, and we probably would not be married. I praise God we are homeowners and are experiencing a very full and prosperous life while giving and serving. We currently serve and worship with Bishop Carl Smith at New Destiny Church in Pittsburg, CA. Through the grace of God, I am blessed to deliver the Word of God to all those who are open to receive it through this book. The enemy still attacks but we know we are already victorious in Jesus' name!

Invitation into the Kingdom

Some women have been through tougher situations than me and have survived through the grace of God. The best advice I can give someone who can relate to any part of my story is to develop an authentic and intimate relationship with God. The Word of God says that you cannot come to the Father except through Jesus, "Jesus answered, 'I am the way and the truth and the life. No one comes to the Father except through me'." John 14:6. To receive Jesus as your personal Lord and Savior it is as simple as believing and repeating this prayer out loud:

"Dear Heavenly Father, you said in your word if we confess our sins, you are faithful and just to forgive us of our sins and cleanse us from all unrighteousness. I confess with my mouth that Jesus is Lord, and I believe in my heart that God raised him from the dead. Jesus, I welcome you into my heart to be the Lord of my life. I receive you as my Lord and Savior. Thank you for saving me."

You are now saved. If that was your first time praying that prayer, then you are what the Bible calls a born-again believer. The next step is to be a part of a Bible-teaching church because we need you to survive. Fellowshipping with other believers will encourage you and support you through life battles. Here are some of my favorite scriptures that have helped me, and will help you on your journey with God as well:

> "Do not give up meeting together, as some are in the habit of doing, but encouraging one another—and all the more as you see the Day approaching." Hebrews 10:25

> "Therefore if any man be in Christ, he is a new creature: old things are passed away; behold, all things are become new." 2 Corinthians 5:17.

> "And God raised us up with Christ and seated us with him in the heavenly realms in Christ Jesus" Ephesians 2:6.

> "After the Lord Jesus had spoken to them, he was taken up into heaven and he sat at the right hand of God." Mark 16:19

I am no longer in the bondage of shame, guilt or self-condemnation. I am free! I sit at the right hand of the Father in heaven through the Lord Jesus Christ. Therefore, since God is on the throne and Jesus Christ is sitting at His right hand; and since I am in Christ, who sits on the throne with God, I sit on the throne as well. I am qualified to reign because my Lord and Savior

Jesus Christ reigns and I am in Him and He is in me. He washed me clean and presents me faultless before the Father! He is the King of kings and the Lord of lords. I declare I am a lady and a lord. I declare I am the righteousness of God. I declare I am worthy of love, peace, healing, prosperity and I am an heir to the promises of God! I shout glory, hallelujah to the Most High God!

Healing wasn't easy, but it was necessary for me to be the woman that I am today. I did three things to get me to where I am, and to start your healing process, you can do the same:

- Receive and accept forgiveness and the gift of salvation from God through Jesus Christ who presents me faultless to God.
- Forgive others who owe me an apology.
- Refocus my attention on first the Kingdom of God believing that God will supply all my needs according to His riches and glory; then took on the action steps I need to take to prepare myself for what God wanted to do in my life.

Knowing what you want will help you align your will with God's Will. What do you want? What do you really want? Write it down, be detailed, and review it daily. Believe and have faith in God and watch God perform miracles in your life! If you can hold it in your mind, then you can hold it in your hand. Proper preparation beats poor performance. Prepare while you wait on your door to open. Your timing and God's timing are not the same. When you really trust God, you will be okay with not receiving what you thought you wanted because you trust that God has your best interest at heart.

In all your ways acknowledge God and He will direct your path. It's not about what you see, it's all about what you believe. Now let's put a praise on it! I love Tash Cobbs song Put a Praise On It: "There's a miracle in this room with my name on it! There's a healing in this room and it's here for me! There's a breakthrough in this room and it's got my name on it so I'm going to put a praise on it. Somebody put a praise on it! Can you help me put a praise on it?!"

Amen and Selah.

From Broken Pieces to God's Masterpiece

Written by Chelle Keith

Heal me, O LORD, and I shall be healed; save me,
and I shall be saved: for thou art my praise.

Jeremiah 17:14

I always thought my life would be filled with love, peace, and happiness with a bit of troubled waters along the way. It was nothing that I couldn't handle because my mother taught me to be strong and that with God, all things are possible. I stood on that and believed it like it was an anthem. Growing up in church all my life, singing in the choir, directing even down to being on the usher board. I grew up knowing and believing in Him and there was no one else I could call on in tough times. He was the yin to my yang.

Don't get me wrong. I tried to party and get with the in-crowd, but I was so out of place.

I had my first child when I was 18 with a much older man. My mother was so disappointed in me because I know she had big dreams for me. But she was determined that she would keep pushing me and that me being a young mother would not deter me from my destiny. With her help and support, I was still able to go to college and pursue my degree. She even went with me for my first year.

I worked full time to support myself and my child. Midway through my junior year, I decided that I wanted to transfer schools because they offered more of what I needed in the field of criminal justice. I had bought my first car so that I could drive back and forth to the campus while still working. I would hang out with my friends in another county sometimes after classes before returning home. The good thing about having a supportive mother is she still allowed me to be a young adult and do things that people my age were doing. Although I had this beautiful baby, I didn't miss any of the things that I wanted to do. I was still responsible but able to be outgoing as well.

One weekend, I was hanging with some friends and was introduced to a mutual friend. I really wasn't interested in him at first but after talking for a minute I was like, *this could go somewhere.* We started to develop a relationship and then I found myself going to his house after school instead of hanging with my other friends. After a few months, I had moved into my apartment and he would come up to visit as well. There was also someone else that I was dealing with so I wasn't sure where this long-distance thing would go. This other guy had made this choice of needing space so even though I was heartbroken with his decision, I went with it and moved on.

Things became serious and before I knew it, we were in a relationship. He moved from where he lived, and we were instantly a family.

Our relationship was progressing, so much so that I became pregnant with my second child. Wow, another one? What was I going to do with another baby? Honestly, I wasn't ready to have another baby. I talked to my sister and after a deep discussion, I decided to have an abortion. I even looked up the number and researched facilities to see where I could have it done and how it could be paid for. After crying, praying, contemplating and doing everything in between, my heart wouldn't let me do it. It was against everything that I stood for.

So, on September 19, 1993, my son was born. This was the most handsome little boy that I had ever seen. He had jet black curly hair and these beautiful brown eyes. His caramel skin was smooth, and he was just perfect. I was so biased because I knew my children were the cutest things on this earth and I loved them. These babies were mine.

I had a newborn and a 3-year-old all before I could blink but it was okay. I could handle it and I didn't mind. We moved into a two-bedroom house near one of my sisters. So, when they weren't in daycare, I could just drop them off to her. My mother would always step in and pick them up or she would take my daughter and my older sister would have my son. My support system was through the roof and we made it work.

While things were starting to fall into place, my relationship was falling apart. Both of us were working full-time jobs and in college. I know it sounds a lot for young adults and we had a lot going on so it was a bit stressful but at the same time, I knew I could handle it. It was no big deal, which was my thought process. After a few months or so, that's when things began to get hectic. A lot of arguments over unnecessary things. It was becoming too much and it got to the point where I wanted out. I was unhappy but I had to be strong for my children. I loved them more than life.

Being in a relationship of uncertainty, working and going to school, I now have these two children, I thought my life was full of chaos. I felt as if I had taken on more than I could handle and there was no sense of normalcy. My young adult life was gone. I had another responsibility and was trying to juggle life as I knew it. It was becoming frustrating but all I could do was lean on family and God. Situations on the home front were going crazy and I didn't know how to put it back in line. I have bills now, rent, utilities, no vehicle. It was all too much for a 25-year-old woman.

The Shift

My life changed on February 3, 1993. It was a day like any other. We walked home from school and I took the baby to his doctor's appointment. He had to get shots so by the time we made it back home, he was cranky. My mom was taking my daughter with her and would come back and get the baby later. There was a jumper that I had placed in the doorway of my kitchen and living room. The baby played in it for a little while, bouncing himself up and down, giving us entertainment. When he wanted out, he would make this crazy noise that was the cutest. He was babbling and trying to say, "Mama," with the slobber sliding down his chin. The smile from my children always warmed my heart and made my day. I picked him up and put him in his walker while my mom and I talked about the rest of the plans for the day. She was coming back to take me to work and would return later to get Devon so that my significant other could do his homework. When we looked over, Devon was moving backward in the walker and already trying to make moves. They grow up so quickly.

I later went on to work and everything seemed to be going normal and as planned. Around 8 or so, my mom came to my job and told my supervisor that there was an emergency at my home, and I needed to leave. When I got into the car, she said she had called to check on the baby and she heard he was crying in the background. She asked what was wrong and was told that he was fussy due to his shots earlier that day. She said that once she and my daughter got out of the tub, she would be over to get him. My mother only lived about 10 minutes away, give or take. She then went on to say that just as she was getting dressed and told him she was on the way, hung up the phone, he immediately called back and said he was taking the baby to the hospital and there was something wrong.

As my mom was telling me this, my heart sank because you never want to hear that something is going on with your children. But I also felt in my heart that something wasn't right. I dropped by the house and I hopped out of the car, running to the door and seeing that it was slighting opened. I called out and no one answered. The TV was still on, but the house was empty. I ran back to the car and we headed to the hospital, praying in my spirit that everything was ok. I kept thinking that maybe he reacted to the shots. That's all I kept saying over and over.

The doctor called us all into a room and gave us the news that my son was gone. He was barely hanging on when he arrived, but they were doing what they could to bring him back. I shut down and was completely broken. You hear horror stories of others all the time and how they felt but when it hits home, it's something different. The emotions are different and hard to explain. I stopped breathing. I went numb and there was nothing that anyone could say to me that would console me. My son, my baby boy was no longer breathing. My life was over. I couldn't even begin to think where to pick up pieces of my life. The doctor order sedatives for me and asked if I wanted to hold him one last time.

I tried to prepare myself as the nurse brought my son into the room with all my family. He was wrapped in a blanket and handed to me. He looked as if he was sleeping. I stroked his black curly hair and sang to him. I gave instructions to the nurse to put his socks on because his feet get cold at night. I wanted to make sure that he was taken care of as if I was dropping him off to the babysitter. I kissed his cheeks and my tears dripped on his forehead. I repeated to him how much I loved him and that he was going to be ok. I didn't want to let him go as my mom and sisters tried to get me to release him from my arms. I was determined to convince myself that he was just asleep. This wasn't real. This wasn't happening to me. It was a dream to hold this baby and think that he wasn't returning home with me.

My sister says she heard this guy in the corner stating, "I killed him. I killed him." But no one was really paying any attention to that. We were all so engaged in saying our last goodbyes. The last thing I remember was being taken home and put in the bed. I was worn out and in a complete fog.

The Truth Hurts

Days later, detectives came to my home wanting to take us uptown for questioning. It was told to my mom that it was just for routine purposes, so she agreed and called my sister to come to the station to be with me. When we arrived, I was placed in one room and he was placed in another. After asking a series of questions, the detective left me alone for a while. I have to say that it was the longest ten minutes of my life. When he returned, he says that my brother and sister had shown up and were in the lobby. He then left me alone again and when he came back, he sat down and let out a sigh. He told me that the man had confessed to killing my son. I was told that he beat him repeatedly in his stomach. Again, here I am left breathless and life has been taken from me.

What do I do with this information? They apparently told my brother and sister as well because I heard him let out this scream that was horrifying before he flipped over the soda machine. It was crazy! My thoughts and feelings were all over the place. I wanted to get to this man and make him feel like I felt. Even though he was arrested, and I knew that he'd have to go to prison, that wasn't enough for me. I wanted to kill him just as he killed my son. My heart was ripped out of my chest.

I can't believe he killed my baby. Are you kidding me? What kind of person would do something like this to a baby? He had to be the devil himself to take away an innocent child. And what is the reason behind it? To hurt me, my family. What? *Why?!* I needed answers but had no way to get them.

I've never felt any type of pain like this. I was sad, hurt, angry. All these emotions were coming to the surface. I began to seek God because I was so angry. I had all these questions.

I began to seek God by praying and keeping a diary of how I felt. Whenever I was angry or started feeling depressed, I would find myself going into prayer and asking my mom to pray for me and give me some direction. I had all of these questions of why would he do this? Why would God allow something like this to happen? Why couldn't He spare my child?

Grieving Through the Motions

It was only when I began to accept what was taken from me, did I find some type of peace and comfort. It took me moving to another state to find that. I was so tired of hearing, "I'm sorry for your loss." It drove me crazy! So, I ran away. It was within the years of my escape that God showed me the situation and how different it could've been. It could've been all three of us, but He spared mine and my daughter's life.

The process of healing and moving forward was hard because I was in a stage of blaming. I was angry at my mom because I felt that she should've taken my son with her. *Why did she take so long to get back to the house?* I was angry at God because I thought I was being punished for something. *What did I do to deserve all this grief?* Then it went to *why not me?* I could've taken the blows. He didn't need to go through any of that.

I couldn't believe that it was my son I saw on that table. I wanted someone to come to me and tell me that this was a mistake. That I could now wake up from this nightmare and kiss my baby boy. But that would never happen again. I expected a miracle at some point. I needed to miraculously release this feeling of heartache. Even though I saw the body and held him, it was still so surreal to me. The sorrow I felt was gut-wrenching. I wanted instant relief; I wanted the pain to be gone. I wanted and needed for God to make it all better.

I found myself resenting my friends who had children. It was affecting my friends on the home front. I knew I was broken at that point because I was so distant and disconnected from everything and everyone. I completely shut down from the world. In my mind, I knew I had a daughter to take care of and I did all that I knew to try to get back to a normal life.

I moved to Maryland and lived on a military base in 1994. I was in a new relationship but also knew that this trial was coming up soon, so I tried to live a normal life and lived well. Even being out of state away from family was hard but I managed. I worked, moved on a military base with my significant other and lived well. I started working for this credit card company in Maryland to keep myself occupied. I would come to visit my mom every other weekend because she would keep my daughter sometimes during the summer. I stayed away for years and then I received the call. The trial date had been set and I would have to come in to testify.

No Justice, No Peace

I was having mixed emotions. I knew this was something I had to prepare myself for, to relive this night all over again. We came to town and the trial began. It only lasted a few days and I wasn't allowed in for the entire week. I took the stand on that Wednesday. I went through the questions, cried my tears and felt myself getting angry all over again. It was emotional. I was devastated to look over in that courtroom and see a face I hadn't seen in months. A face that destroyed my whole world. The face that took my baby boy away from me. My son, born September 19 and gone February 3. How crazy is that? Now I have to look at this dude, who looked as if he had no remorse. It was like he didn't feel bad at all. No expression whatsoever. I was angry and wanted to lash out. I felt the same way I felt the night they told me that my son was gone. I was numb and began to get nauseous. I hated him and wanted him to die, just as my son did.

At the end of the week, the prosecuting attorney asked if I could sit in on the last day. They were going sentence him immediately so she thought I should at least be able to be available. The judge agreed and I came in and sat next to my family. He began to talk, and the attorneys gave their closing arguments. It was then that I heard the severity of my son's injuries. I guess it was the not knowing that made some things easy but hearing the details hit me like a ton of bricks. My son was beaten like a grown man, laid on a pillow and hit in his stomach repeatedly. According to his autopsy, his liver was like jelly.

My God! What do you *do* with that information?

And now the sentence.

As I listened to everything they said this man did to my son, I don't know how I stayed in my seat. My mind was racing back to moments that would give me clues that he was capable of doing something so cruel to my child. I saw signs but never acknowledged them. Such as days before he passed, my son had a black eye. He was scheduled to take pictures days after so it wasn't visible, but you could still see it a little. I had asked how it happened. He said my daughter was jumping on the bed and he rolled off. Well, I knew that wasn't true because anytime my daughter did something wrong, she immediately would start to apologize to avoid getting spanked. Then the story changed to he was bouncing him on his knee, and he slipped. I didn't feel right with the answers that I was getting. I as his mother should've known.

After closing arguments, the jury went out to deliberate and it was only a few hours before they had reached a decision. Life with mercy. Again, my heart sank, and we were all disgusted. This meant that he would be eligible for parole after so many years. Another punch in the gut and I felt as if justice was not on my side. This wasn't fair and not enough punishment for me. He still has a chance at life while my son doesn't.

Unbelievable! I was so messed up and didn't understand this process. Who are the people who make these decisions? Did they not hear all this evidence? What this man did to my baby? I couldn't believe this was happening.

I went back home to Maryland disappointed. Once again, numb at the fact that justice was not served enough for me. I shielded my daughter more than usual and became more protective than ever. I didn't trust anyone. It was hard for me to allow anyone in my inner circle. I prayed more for God to give me some relief, to heal my heart and let me be able to maintain my sanity.

My relationship started to become more of an effort to hold together. I looked at him differently. I wanted things to work but yet came up with different excuses to push him away. I would start arguments for no reason. The love I was receiving made no sense to me. I was damaged so why would he want to be with me? I began to question his love. Eventually, I packed my things and left, moving to West Virginia with my daughter and starting over.

My Breakthrough Moment

One day while speaking with my mom, I made the decision that I needed and wanted to heal from this moment of feeling lost. I know she and others prayed for me, but I had to do some sincere, heart to heart praying myself. Not like the usual prayers that were halfhearted and just to get through the day. I wanted my *life* back.

My relationship was destroyed because I allowed certain things to distract what I knew was good. It was sabotage. I moved back home for a while thinking that this was what would be best. My dreams still haunted me. I moved through life as if I had no purpose. I went through the motions.

My trust issues and hurt caused a lot of problems and confusion in my relationship. Because I wasn't willing to let another man in, I pushed away some amazing men out of fear. I missed out on being able to heal and love again. All that was left to cling to was my daughter. Then once she graduated from high school, she too was gone. She got a full-ride scholarship and moved to Atlanta. I was excited but also sad because I knew that I'd be alone. I had a house built but no one left to fill it but me and my things. I developed this OCD and obsession with online shopping and shoe fetish to fill the void. That was my new comfort.

Years had gone by and I now lived in Atlanta. I placed my home on the market for rent and decided to be closer to my daughter. She had been asking me to move for some time and I was there all the time anyway so why not? Still thinking that my life was normal and back with my now-husband, I again, broke the rules and pushed him away. After months of being separated, he left again and returned to the west coast. I recall a conversation he and I had which entailed of him telling me that only until I confront this person and the demons head-on, will I ever have a successful relationship.

Although I didn't want to admit this, he was right. I agreed to do this when the time was right. Of course, my immediate family and church family were always supportive, but his words meant something different because we had so much history. He knew me inside and out.

One day I was in my room and my mind drifted off to my son. I was thinking about how my daughter and he would be at the age they were. I found the courage to do something that had been on my mind. I scrolled through Facebook and did a name search. And there it was. The name and face that I dreaded to see. I saw that he had been released and now has a son.

Immediately tears filled my eyes and I began to get hot. *How could God allow Him the opportunity to raise a son when he took mine? How do you get to have that experience when I was robbed of it? Was this God's way of punishing him?* So many questions and not enough answers. While I didn't have the answers, I did know one thing to be true: Every time he looks at his son, he has to think of the life he took. That was my way of being rational. Although it may have been rational, it still hurt me to my core.

I called my niece crying. I was so upset. She was my ride or die, so I knew she would understand how I was feeling. We go hard for each other and when I needed someone to go along with my mood, she was the one I called. After speaking with her, I sat in my bathroom and I begin to think of what I needed to do. Should I send this message? If so, what should I say? I wanted to know the answers to all of the questions that I had been thinking on for 26 years. He had to give me something and he owed me that if nothing else. I went to work and on my way home I asked God what to do and begin to type the message. I backed out a couple of times, but God spoke and said this is your opportunity.

So I finished the message and hit send. I began to shake, and a cold feeling came all over me. Within a matter of seconds, I could see him responding.

Forgiveness Leads to Healing

I wanted to know the full details of what took place that night. I thought back to the conversation of me needing to talk to him for some resolution. So, one day on my home from work, I sent him a message. I typed, erased and typed again. I closed my eyes, said a prayer and believe it or not, God gave me the words to say. They were simple. I looked down saw that he was online. The comment bubbles appeared, showing that he started typing. My heart was beating so hard, it felt like it was about to pop out of my chest. He responded to my message, but the answer I received wasn't good enough. I don't know why but I needed details. It felt like a cop-out answer and I needed something better than what I got. He then asked if I could give him a call. I hesitated but heard God say that this was my opportunity to get what I was seeking. I waited a bit then called. Just to hear the voice from years ago was creepy but I had to endure it. He told me everything. My heart was closing as I listened to every word. The visuals that were going on inside my head was too vivid. And once he was done, I sat in silence, trying to allow it to process.

Once I let out a sigh of relief, I had to ask for forgiveness. It wasn't for him but for me. Hate had been eating at me like a cancer. All these years, I thought I was good because I had asked God to forgive me. But I was yet holding on to the one thing that kept me from being completely free. I now knew that it wasn't him that was blocking my blessings, but it was me. My feelings, my spoken and unspoken thoughts were standing in the way of me living the life that God wanted me to have.

What changed the trajectory of my life was when I heard God's voice. He spoke to me and said that it was time to move on and He had equipped me to help others. His voice was so clear and plain. It was then that I knew I was strong enough, so I started working on my ministry, Broken Pieces. There are so many men and women who have gone through either the same thing or something similar. And I knew all too well how it feels to be alone during seasons of brokenness. I wanted to help people heal and become strong so they too can move forward in their purpose.

My life is so different now because I have healed and forgave. I can now breath and enjoy life and my family. My daughter and my grandson are my world. Everyone who has crossed my path has been such a blessing to me. My relationships have been mended and I've learned to love again, freely.

Resilience is Key

My advice to any woman or man who has experienced this situation would be to let them know that they can and will survive. Prayer changes things and through God, you can get through any struggle, heartache, pain, obstacle, whatever the situation. Through prayer, acceptance, and forgiveness, life will change. Let people help you. Be open with others and don't shut down. The things we go through, we may not see it then but it's necessary. Everything we go through is necessary. God has a plan and a purpose for our life, and He will never leave us or forsake us. We may feel as if we're out in the middle of the ocean with no lifesaver, God is there. There is healing in the power of prayer. Listen to the voices of reason. It may feel and seem like the end, but you can survive. I promise.

Getting to A Life of "More"

Written by Callandra Smith

"As soon as I pray, you answer me; you encourage me by giving me strength."
Psalm 138:3

I remember being a young child and knowing that I would enjoy providing a product or service to others for money. I was always creating something. I am a creative person and I live and breathe creativity. From creating and directing commercials in my parents' living room to creating hair bows for little girls, I knew from an early age I wanted to create and get paid for it. At the time, I did not have a formal name for the desire to create and get paid for it, but I knew it was something that was a must for me.

I would later learn that the desire to create and get paid for my creations is known as the entrepreneurial spirit. The entrepreneurial spirit was something I was born with. I did not read to acquire it. I did not seek it out of envy for what someone else had. It was something that was in me from birth. It was my entrepreneurial spirit that sparked my desire for wanting more out of life, but I had to go through A LOT of changes before entrepreneurship became a reality.

I remember being a child, maybe eight or nine years old and getting roller skates for Christmas. I remember going outside and roller-skating up and down the street for fun with my childhood friend. We would roller skate for hours. It was good exercise for our legs and so freeing to be gliding in the wind.

Prior to getting my roller skates at the age of eight, I had classical dance training in the genres of ballet and tap since the age of two. I love ballet and love to utilize it every time I have the opportunity. Armed with the desire to choreograph a classical number and with the entrepreneurial spirit, I thought it would be a grand idea to perform a synchronized roller-skating routine for my neighbors and charge them twenty-five cents to witness it. I do not remember if we had music to accompany our routine. Nonetheless, I was ready and excited about creating and making money. I presented this idea to my friend. She liked it and our quest to become performers was becoming a reality. We came up with a routine. We practiced our routine and we set out to make money from our craft. After knocking on doors, we made $1.50 altogether. This meant each one of us would walk away with 75¢. That was so exhilarating. One of the neighbors was so impressed with our synchronized roller skate number that she gave us a tip. How about that? My entrepreneurial spirit was being fed and it felt good.

As time went along, I acquired more creative skills. I took classes and was around people in my family who would encourage creativity. I explored the creative world as much as I could.

I loved having creative skills and the entrepreneurial spirit, but something was happening. Life was happening. I grew into an adult and needed to have money to pay my monthly bills. I had no confidence in my ability to manage my own official money-making business nor did I feel like I had any skills that I could offer to paying clients and customers. All I knew is that I needed money and a job was the place to earn it, so after college, I entered the workforce and became an employee.

My very first job while in college and immediately after college was a retail job. I enjoyed it. I enjoyed learning customer service skills and how to work a point of sale machine. Finding awesome gifts was another benefit to working this job. Because I was responsible for my department by keeping merchandise in its proper location, I was able to get very familiar with the products in my department and which items were on sale. Meeting new people was also another highlight of this job.

I was content with my job and everything was going well. I do remember my feet would hurt so badly while I was working this retail job. No matter how hard or how long I looked for shoes, I could not find any shoes that would alleviate the aching in my feet. I knew I would not make it long-term in this retail position with my feet hurting like they were, but I hung in there and stayed at the job.

After a few years of working in this retail position, something happened inside of me. I began to get bored and tired of the job. I wanted more. At the time, I did not know what the "more" was or how to get it. I just knew it was time for something different.

I have to clarify that at the beginning of my quest for "more", I had no knowledge of anything regarding my purpose, or God-given assignment. All I knew is that I had a desire to have a life that was bigger than what I was currently living. I also knew how to pray to God and ask Him for His direction in my life. Because I invited God into my decision-making process, I know without a shadow of a doubt that my hunger for "more" and my willingness to pay attention to what God was doing in and through me throughout the years is was what kept me going when times were tough.

Yes, there were PLENTY of rough times in my personal and professional life. At the time, it did not always feel like God was with me or that I would actually get to a place of seeing the life of "more" I so strongly desired. In retrospect, I can see that God was ordering my steps throughout the entire time. He was making sure that all roads led to the place of "more".

There were many times I came to a crossroads and had to make some decisions on which way to go and which open door to walk through. I can, now, see that God was there the whole time. It was God who took my decisions and ensured I learned all the necessary life lessons and skills I needed to learn to get me to the next place in life which would eventually lead me to my "more".

The Work

My second job was with a luxury retailer. At the luxury retailer, I worked a desk job where I was responsible for inputting data from the buyers' office into the company computer system. The job I had was very important, as the entire online structure of the organization revolved around my department. Although we worked a lot of long hours, I enjoyed this job because it allowed me the opportunity to see some of the finer, luxurious goods available on the market. I was living the dream of working around so many beautiful items. I got to model a beautiful silk pantsuit for the launch of the annual Christmas catalog. I also got to attend some photoshoots where pictures of items were being taken for upcoming catalogs. Even with all this excitement, I eventually came to a place where I was longing for more in life. There were some high and low points, but I could not see myself in this position for the rest of my life. When the time was right, I moved on to the next position.

At this time, I still do not know what it is I am seeking. All I know is that I am wanting to get to a life of "more". I have to fulfill this unrelenting desire. I began asking God where he wanted me to be. He put it on my mind to join a temp agency. I was able to quickly find work with the temp agency using the same skills I had acquired on my second job. I noticed, after some time, that I kept getting placed in data entry positions. It was repetitive and I was not growing. I was not going in the direction of "more" on the jobs I was being placed. I had to make a change.

I went home one night and updated my resume. While updating my resume, I realized a lot of skills were transferrable. The next day, I went to my temp agency staffing manager and presented my current skills and knowledge base to her. I asked if I could be placed in positions with more responsibility using the skills I had acquired in previous jobs. She was very attentive and compassionate and began asking questions. She could see, after talking to me, that I did have some skills that could be used in the jobs they had available. She said she would give me a chance to take on more responsibility on my temp assignments. Soon after, I began being placed in receptionist positions. Boy was I in my element! I loved being a receptionist. I was around people. I was helping people and I was using the skills I had acquired on previous jobs in a different capacity. My world was expanding!

Now, I was at a place where God had equipped me with the ability to know how to speak up for myself and showcase what I have to offer. I was learning how to use my current skill set but in different capacities. I was learning and I was growing. Yes, I had to make the decisions on whether or not to accept a certain opportunity, but after I prayed and made the decision I thought was best for me at the time, God did His part and ensured that, along the way, I got the tools I needed to move on to the next stage in life.

After some time at the temp agency, my confidence and my skill set began to grow. God had even placed some people in my pathway to be kind to me and help me along in my journey toward "more". Yes, I was working on jobs, but that entrepreneurial spirit would often rise inside of me and would not go away. The amazing thing to me is that, at this point, the puzzle pieces were all starting to come together to form a bigger picture. I could see it. Life was starting to make sense. Thankfully, God knew all along what He had planned for me and was working with me to get there.

The Transformation

I could begin to see how God was putting people in my life that would help feed both endeavors - my job and my entrepreneurial spirit. He blessed me with a manager who encouraged me to start my own business while I was working. This manager would teach me how to use my time and money to pursue my creative passions. I began making floral corsages and mosaic art. She was one of my biggest supporters at the time. I had people rooting for me and it felt exciting to be working a job and working on my business on the side.

There was another lady who was my manager on my temp job who really touched my heart. We were about the same age, but she was responsible for approving my time and training me. I had been on the temp assignment for a while and had become a part of the team. The people there were so nice and showered me with so much love on my birthday.

This particular manager and I would sometimes talk about some of our goals. I told her I was wanting to get a camcorder (yes, this was before smartphones) so I could record events. I did not know she remembered some of the goals I told her until one day she came to me to let me know that my assignment would be ending soon and that if I wanted that video camera, now would be the time to purchase it. Needless to say, I purchased the video camera and was so grateful that she had the heart to help me along the way. It was at this point that it was starting to dawn on me that I should be more intentional with my time and money to ensure they were getting me to the life of "more" I was seeking. No, I did not know exactly what the "more" was, but I was just starting to notice commonalities in life patterns and supernatural thought processes that began to capture my attention.

While working at the temp agency, I worked my creative business on the side. My business was heavily supported by my relatives and friends. I was thankful for their support, but I knew I would need to get my business in front of people I did not know. I did not know how to do this and to be honest, I believe God had some additional skills and life lessons He wanted me to learn before He entrusted me with a full-fledged business. After taking some time off from working the temp agency and trying to work my creative business, the money began to run out. I was at the place where I needed to find another job. I was not excited about re-entering the workforce, but I was obedient.

I sought out a job and secured a position in the finance industry - insurance to be exact. Once again, I was able to use the skills I had gained in my previous jobs on my new job but yet again in a different capacity. In addition, I learned so much about houses. I learned the parts of a house and basically how to rebuild a house if necessary. I didn't think I would get to use my creative skills in this position, but I had the opportunity to design houses in computer-aided design software and that experience was pretty cool.

As you can see, my technical skills were growing. With each job, I was able to learn something new that added to my current skill set. Each job I worked helped me to broaden my current knowledgebase which then spilled over into in my personal life. I noticed I was growing professionally and personally. Who knew taking jobs that did not feed my creative passion would help me grow as a person? I certainly did not, but it is evident that God did.

The Revelation

I was born a people person, but I noticed my communication skills began to sharpen and my planning skills began to improve. These were two skills that were heavily utilized and developed on my jobs, but they were proving to be an asset to me in my personal life and my pursuit of more. I was starting to see that these qualities would help serve me later down the line. It was around this time that God showed me what my "more" was. He began to make it very clear through interactions I was having and gut feelings what my "more" was. When I realized what my "more" was, I was so excited.

Believe it or not, I was already operating in my "more" way before my epiphany. I was operating in my "more" as a child. I was operating in my "more" all along. I was in a place where I could not see my "more" because God had to take me on a journey. The reason I believe God did not make my "more" crystal clear to me in the beginning stages of this journey is because He knows I would have been more focused on trying to fully operate in my "more" before it was time. It was not, yet, what God wanted me to focus on. My job at the time was to learn the technical skills and life lessons God had for me so that I could continue to grow and progress. My job was to grow in knowledge and faith.

My "more" is to help others learn and grow while running a business. It is that simple. Yes, my "more" entails combining my love for people and my entrepreneurial spirit. I also get to help uplift, empower, and encourage people with my creative skills. When I look back over the chain of events in my life, everything I went through was leading up to my "more." I was pursuing my creative passion. I was learning the ins and outs of running a business, and I was also helping everyone I could with an encouraging word. If you come to me with a problem, you do not just get to dump your problems on me and continue to be in the same place with the same mindset in six months or a year. There should be some type of growth (spiritual or mental), be it small or exponential. All who know me know I am going to share some information, tips, and tools on how you can move out of your current place into a more pleasant next phase of life.

When I realized what my "more" was, I was so relieved. The "more" I was searching for and the "more" that kept nudging at me throughout the years was what others call purpose. Some may call it my God-given assignment. Now I know it was God who was beckoning me with the gut-feelings and nudging's to get up and follow Him into a life of "more". It was God who was guiding me and making sure all along the way that I was accumulating knowledge and information I can take forward with me into my future of "more."

There were so many life lessons God taught me along the way. Some of the lessons were:

- There will be some losses during the journey. Some of the losses will be financial while others are cherished family members and friends.

- My help will not come from people I know. My help will come from people I do not know. God always has someone in position who will follow His directions to help you when needed.
- Some people will choose to no longer spend time with me when they realize that the way I plan to spend my time will be different from theirs.
- People will tell me and try to get the point across that I am not good enough to fit within their circle.
- Though I had been born and raised in church, God was going to put me in situations where all of the scriptures I learned as a child would begin to have a special meaning to me.
- The blessing I am asking for will take years to show up.
- I will see the best and fastest change in my situation when I am obedient to the direction and directives God gives me along the way.
- I will get tired of waiting. I will feel hopeless as a result.
- There will be times when I will not be able to talk to anyone about what is troubling me. People will either have their own

problems or will not understand the problems I present to them.

- It will take a lot of work to get to where I am trying to go.
- I will have to finish the first task God put in my heart and mind to complete before He gives me new or more instructions.
- The journey will not be easy, but it will be gratifying, nonetheless.

This list by no means scratches the surface of the lessons God had for me to learn during my journey of seeking "more." There is no way I can share all God taught me over the years while going through this process. I will share with you that some of the scriptures that kept me encouraged throughout my journey of seeking "more" and what they meant to me. They were:

1. **Romans 12:2**

    I had to learn that even though I have a huge family, know a lot of people, and have a church family, none of them were going to get me to my point of "more". Getting to more was a journey I was going to have to take on my own. No one else could take the journey for me. No one else could take the journey with me. God made sure it was just He and I on the journey so that no one else got the credit. God made sure to remove a lot of distractions in my life so I can focus and hear solely from Him without doubt. In other words, God had to renew my mind so I could fully see and fully hear from him. He had to change my perspective and mindset so that I could operate in the purpose He had predestined for me.

2. **Romans 12:8**

   I remember reading this scripture and being so excited because I felt like I finally found myself in scripture. There was something in the Bible that acknowledged me, and it had to do with my spiritual gifts. One of them is the gift of exhortation. I am an encourager at heart and will encourage you into better if you stay around me long enough.

3. **Psalm 30:5 (second half)**

   Yes, there were a lot of times I did not understand what was going on in my life or where I was headed. I was scared and hopeless, but there was always that feeling of no longer wanting to cry after crying for a little while. The desire to cry was supernaturally replaced with hope. The desire to give up was replaced with new instructions and new ideas from God. Weeping did not endure for long. There was always work for me to get up and do.

4. Psalm 138:3
   After I was further along in the process, there were times when I would pray and would immediately get an answer. There were times when I would cry or be hopeless and I would get the supernatural surge of strength.

I had no idea when I asked God for more in my professional career that He would put me on a journey that would help to grow me and mature me both professionally and personally. The journey was not a straight shot. There were a lot of detours, long waits, and last-minute changes. Although God is still developing me into a full-time entrepreneur, I am finally getting to that place where I know I am operating in my "more" – my God-given assignment and I am so thankful for it.

My prayer is that you have been encouraged by my life experiences presented in this story. I pray that if you read something in this story that resembles your current place in life, you will be encouraged to know that better is coming. Keep going. It is not over for you. You will have to go through some rough patches, but when it is all said and done, you will look back and understand why you had to go through what you went through.

Pardon Me, Post - You're Defeated!

Written by Hope Marr

The righteous cry, and the Lord heareth, and delivereth them out of all their troubles. The Lord is nigh unto them that are of a broken heart; and saveth such as be of a contrite spirit.

Psalm 34:17-18 (KJV)

I was pregnant expecting my first child at 31 years old. I thought I would never have any children and I was alright with that until I felt her kicking. The first time I felt her kick, I was in my fifth or sixth month of pregnancy. She was not a very active baby prior to this day. I was sitting in the living room and all of a sudden, she started squirming around and I could actually feel her moving! I ran into the bedroom and said David feel my stomach. I placed his hand where I felt her moving and we both looked at each other and just smiled. She ended up on the left side of my stomach for almost 2 days. That was very uncomfortable when trying to sleep. But it was one of the greatest moments during my pregnancy.

My family and friends were more excited than I was of the news that I was expecting. After I accepted the fact that I was pregnant I was looking forward to my first child. It was a challenging pregnancy with being sick all day and night. I still can't figure out why they call it "morning sickness" when it lasted almost the entire time during my pregnancy. I enjoyed the bond between my fiancé and me during my pregnancy more than anything. We were excited to attend every doctor's appointment and see the growth with each visit. The day we found out we were having a girl was amazing. My father wanted a boy because we have more females than males in our family. I think my dad felt alone being around emotional women all the time.

I was in constant prayer that God would remove this morning sickness so I could enjoy my pregnancy. I wanted to enjoy eating hamburgers, ice cream and pickles like most pregnant women talked about. That wasn't my story, I needed salt to keep from throwing up all day and water when it stayed down. But, with God by my side, I kept pushing through.

I remember asking my mom, "How did you turn out to be a great mom?" I was scared I would fail as a new mom. My mom said, "Once you see her it will all come to you naturally." When she said that I thought *I pray that it happens that way for me.*

Our daughter was two weeks overdue, so my delivery was scheduled to be induced. We were nervous and excited at the same time! I remember going down to delivery and feeling scared like never before. I didn't know what to expect but was so happy to have my fiancé by my side. I remember getting the anesthesia because I had to have a C-section performed due to her heart rate dropping during each contraction. I could feel them tugging to pull her out without pain of course. I don't remember much after hearing her cry for the first time.

Life before giving birth was completely different for me. After I had our daughter, my life was forever changed. I was no longer the woman I used to be. Unlike most first-time moms, I did not immediately feel emotionally connected to my baby. I had no idea what was wrong with me. I just thought I was afraid of my new responsibility. I had cared for my goddaughter since she was around two weeks old. I mean I took her everywhere with me, dressed her, doctor appointments and on dates. So, this wasn't my first rodeo when it came to children, so why was I so afraid of being around my child?

When it was time for my daughter to be fed, I remember the nurse asking me, "Do you want to feed your baby?" I wanted to, but I was just afraid I would make a mistake. I would always make up an excuse as to why I couldn't feed her. I only asked the nurse to bring her to my room when the family was coming to see us. Right after they left, I requested the nurse to come and take her back to the nursery. One time I heard a baby crying when the nurse was checking my vitals. I asked whose baby is crying. She said, "Yours, she's just being fussy. Would you like to hold her?" I said, "No, my pain medicine is kicking in now."

Looking back I showed so many signs of something being off. I was certainly not acting like myself. No one said anything about my change in behavior, and after five days in the hospital, I was sent home with my new baby girl. I was scared of the lifetime responsibility of another person. I found myself thinking about dying and not being here to enjoy my baby girl. Never thoughts of hurting her or myself just sad and feeling distant.

Introduction to Mommy-hood

I remember when we first came home from the hospital, David and I would take turns holding her as she slept. Jordan would sleep laying on our chest instead of her crib. After a while, she knew instantly when would put her in her crib because she wouldn't feel our heartbeat. I never wanted to hear her cry. After some time, I knew I would have to get over that so I could clean, cook and anything else that needed to be done. I felt closer to her being home with me instead of in the hospital. I loved dressing her in cute and matching outfits every day. I would wake up day after day with the worst chest pain that went on for months and then headaches followed that. I would go to so many different hospitals thinking I was having a heart attack or something fatal was wrong with me. They would always say, "You are fine just go home and get some rest." I became afraid of being home alone with my baby in case something happened to me.

Five months had gone by, and I still hadn't returned to work. I woke up every day, took a Motrin 800 in an attempt to sleep and remove the chest discomfort I'd wake up, take a couple of deep breaths, and wait to see if my feelings changed. I still had a heaviness in my chest that would never leave and the headaches. I knew nothing had changed.

I had been so worried and anxious that I messed up the lining in my stomach. I had no idea the damage you can do to your body from worrying. I felt like a different person with no understanding of what was going on with me. I stopped singing my gospel songs that used to give me so much joy. I stopped going to church because I had been praying but God didn't answer me. I felt like He abandoned me and our relationship. I was tormented by fear and no sign of it ending soon. I felt like I was missing so many good times with my baby girl. I don't remember much while in the hospital far as bonding time with her. I remember holding her but not feeling like a new mom should have felt. I wanted to get to know her and hold her close to me while in the hospital, but I just couldn't.

I know I was getting on my fiancé and family's nerves with my constant complaints about how I was feeling and wanting them to be with me all the time. All my thoughts were negative and bad, with no joy or thoughts of happiness anymore. It was a heaviness and darkness that I can't begin to explain.

The devil was after my mind and I had no idea how to defeat him. This was an attack that I had never experienced before. Of all the battles and victories this by far was the most challenging. I remember my pastor would always say, "If the devil gets your mind the body will follow." He used to preach about that in church, but I didn't hold on to it too much until it happened to me. I remember my pastor saying that you might not need this message today, but just keep living. When I'm reminded of his words, it tells me that there is nothing new under the sun and this was war!

I recall going to Washington Hospital Center with my mom and we were there all day. This was probably the 7th hospital I went to for months. Finally, I was admitted and spoke with a doctor who told me there was nothing wrong with me. He said, "You have anxiety and you need to do some exercises that will help you relax." Again, I felt discouraged. I knew something deeper than anxiety was wrong with me, and not one doctor could properly diagnose me. I was frustrated because I wanted help and couldn't seem to find any.

I started having problems in my relationship because I didn't want my fiancé to go anywhere once he came home from work. I felt like he was living, and I wasn't. I could not shut my mind off from over-thinking. The only time my mind was quiet was when I was sleeping. My mind never stopped wandering about any and everything. It just wouldn't quit speaking negative things for nothing. I felt as if I was being tormented.

I was at my parents' house one day and my cousin called me on the phone. As we were talking, she asked, "What is wrong with you?" I began to tell her how I had been feeling and what thoughts I was having. I told her how I would wake up thinking, this is the day that I am going to die. I cry as I type this because it brings it all back like it was yesterday.

When I told her this she said, "Oh no! I know exactly what is wrong with you. I am on my way over there now!" She hung up without saying bye and I was sitting there like, *how does she know and none of the doctors in the DMV have a clue.* She came over and said, "Get your shoes so we can go for a ride." We left and as she was driving, she asked me more questions. I didn't tell all my thoughts because how can somebody who proclaim to love Jesus have the thoughts that I had at the time. I couldn't for the life of me understand where those thoughts came from when they were against my God. How can I, the one who loves Him with all my heart have these ungodly thoughts? I was embarrassed and ashamed of myself. I felt condemned every day by Satan.

I learned later that just because I think something, doesn't mean I have to take ownership! Especially if it's not in my heart. The devil with his crafty and sneaky ways will play on your weakness and have you thinking all kinds of crazy things that are NOT true nor are they your character.

My cousin began to tell me that she had gone through anxiety before and some of the symptoms and experiences she went through. After speaking with her and relating to some of her symptoms and thoughts, I began to Google my symptoms. I began to see the symptoms of postpartum and how it affects moms and their relationship with their baby.

According to the American Brain Society, postpartum depression is a mood disorder that affects women soon after they give birth. The disorder is categorized by anxiety, sadness, sleep difficulties, fatigue, or other signs of a low mood. The symptoms are so severe that they interfere with the mother's daily functioning and her ability to care for her child.

Postpartum! I never thought this was the issue I was facing, but it made sense. Quite a few women who give birth experience this issue. I wonder why the doctors didn't check for this considering how I acted during my five day stay in the hospital.

My cousin gave me a CD that was in her car by Marvin Sapp called *I Believe.* She said this song got her through and it would do the same for me. I was willing to try anything. I just wanted to go back to being myself again. At this point, I hadn't been listening to my gospel music, but I was praying off and on again. I started listening to the CD and singing along to the lyrics until I began to believe it for my life. I would play it over and over until I felt a little better. My Pastor would often tell us to remove the spirit of heaviness, we'd have to replace it with the spirit of praise! That's what I started to do. But you know the devil will not let you go that easy. He comes back seven times stronger.

I went back to church with her one day and my mind was so noisy that I couldn't sit in the sanctuary anymore. I signaled my cousin to come to the ladies' room with me for a moment. When she came in behind me, I said, "I just need my mind to be quiet! Help me!" She ran out and got one of the ministers in the church. She told her what was going on and she began to whisper in my ear the word of God. She spoke directly to the devil and I began to praise God in the ladies' room. She told me to read Psalm 40 every day, more than once if I needed to until a change would come. I began doing that every day and I still listened to the song my cousin gave me, even though things remained the same.

Even though the symptoms continued, by reading Psalm 40 daily it allowed me to let go of my hurt, disappointment and even some anger towards my God. People don't like to admit being angry with God because we are told we are not supposed to be. I have been angry two times in my life I recall with my God. Once when I was 18 and my grandfather died. I had no understanding of why a good person would have to die painfully. And of course, while going through Postpartum (self-diagnosed) and feeling like my prayers were being ignored. When Jesus said, "Father why hast thou forsaken me," I can only imagine how he felt. Jesus was perfect, I am not. But I know the pain of calling on a powerful Father who is able to do exceedingly and abundantly above anything you can ask Him for, and you feel like He has left your side. I felt alone and I didn't understand why God didn't answer me in one of my darkest hours. I had heard of Postpartum but never knew anyone personally who experienced this before, so I didn't know how to bring myself out of it.

Encountering Anxiety

I remember September 11, 2001, when the world trade centers were destroyed. I woke up that morning to get ready for work. I got our daughter together for daycare and left our apartment. After strapping her in I said, "Jordan, today is not gonna be a good day to go to work." I felt like something was not right. I stopped by my mother's house, which was only about a mile away. We were there maybe fifteen minutes and the first plane hit the trade center. I grabbed my daughter and ran downstairs in the basement. My mom said, "What are you doing down there?" I was praying to God saying please don't let us die, I just had my baby. I tell you... From that moment on, things just continued to spiral out of control.

I was fearful of almost everything. Having Postpartum eventually turned into (I want to keep anxiety and depression here). I have never had anything like this happen to me in my life.

Even with relationship break ups or losing family or friends, nothing else tormented me like what was sent by Satan to destroy me. I felt all alone because no one knew how or what to do to help me. I felt like I was getting on everyone's nerves. I could see their frustration and how I was weighing them down with my depression. They were still treating me like the old Hope when in fact she was nowhere to be found. They couldn't understand why I didn't want to go home by myself nor drive certain places anymore. I didn't feel comfortable driving far away from home in case something happened. I had no idea what was going on with me or how to get back to being myself and be a happier mommy to my baby girl.

I appreciate my sister, Shannon, more than she will ever know. No matter what is going on in my life, she is always there for me. During my postpartum, she would bathe me when I didn't have the energy to do it myself. That and so many other situations we've shared are the glue that keeps our bond so special.

Despite not getting better, I kept on reading Psalm 40 and going to church. I went to my primary care doctor and explained what was going on with me and he prescribed me some medication for depression. I took the pills home and said, "God, I am not taking these pills." I felt like if I took them, I was relying on the pills and not on God to deliver me. I put them in my dresser drawer and never took one. I kept going to church and listening to the word of God. I listened to it at work all day every day. If you could ever overdose on the word, I would have done so. I couldn't read or listen to enough of the Word to get out of this pit. I listened in my car driving to and from work. Nothing else mattered. I prayed and cried and after that, I cried and prayed some more. I was on my face with the Lord daily with no change. Nothing makes you spend more time with the Lord than pain and despair. I was sick and tired of myself and wanted to be healed. I felt like a dark cloud had surrounded me and all I could do was look out but not get out.

Anxiety is tiring! You are fighting your thoughts daily and trying not to believe what your mind is saying to you. Depression makes you feel exhausted and tiring as well, it makes you sleepy after you already slept for hours. It makes you sad and frustrated you can't do what you really want to do. I remember coming home from work sitting in my favorite chair and not doing anything I said I wanted to do for myself. Some of my family would get mad at me for not doing things they asked of me. I've been told I was selfish when I wouldn't keep my word if I said I would do something.

The truth of the matter was, I didn't have what I needed for myself, so I was not able to give anything to anyone else. It's something when your closest village does not understand what you may be going through. Most times I couldn't explain how I was feeling without sounding crazy. I was scared and worried about what could happen and not what has happened. But, I'm so grateful to my God. In spite of how I felt, thought or even acted at times, He never let go of me.

God Became My Refuge

I kept reading and studying to show myself approved. I couldn't give up after all He has done for me, even though I felt like doing so. It didn't make sense that He would help me like He has in the past to just leave me now. So, I had to learn how to take my thoughts captive. I've read that several times but never knew how to do it. It simply meant just because you think something, you don't have to meditate on it. I learned to replace it with a Godly thought and don't take ownership of the thought. I didn't feel in my heart what I was thinking so I learned to take that thought captive immediately!

I had to learn how to surrender to the Lord. Surrender all my concerns and not have a plan A or B just in case it didn't happen when I wanted something to. That was a hard thing to do for me and sometimes it shows back up in my life. Jeremiah 29:11 became one of my favorite scriptures. It taught me that the Lord only has good plans for me and not of evil or harm. So, if you are hearing thoughts of evil and not for your good it's from Satan. There was so much condemnation on me that it was a battle to pray with expectancy while thinking thoughts that were not of God. I felt like I was not worthy of His goodness or mercy when condemnation was present all the time. Again, more lies from the devil to keep you in fear and bondage.

Psalm 24 was my refuge because it reminded me that my God is mighty in battle! Who is the king of glory, strong and mighty, mighty in battle. I had to stop trying to defeat this demonic attack with my mind. Faith comes by hearing the word of God. I had to begin talking to myself by saying God's promises aloud. When a thought comes that is not of God, I speak to it immediately! You have to have the word of God in you in order to speak it when you are under attack. I realized that this battle was not going to just go away. I think of all my time in church and listening to it on the radio, TV or going to revivals as my Training Camp. I had no idea then that I would need everything I ever learned about God to fight this battle.

I often compare my depression and anxiety to the story of the woman with the issue of blood. I would say her issued lasted 12 years, who am I to complain? Then I exceeded her time with my issue and began to ask God, how long Lord. Why haven't you delivered me? I had a minister that taught beginners class at my church years ago Minister Palmer. He would always reference this scripture, "when I would do good evil is always there" Romans 7:19-21. I can still hear his voice today with such boldness and conviction.

Before I had my daughter, I learned to trust God in the area of my enemies. I learned to trust God to guide me in the right direction. I learned to trust God to make my crooked paths straight. I learned that God will provide my every need. I learned that I don't need no rocks to cry out for me, I will praise Him in the middle of whatever is going on until my change comes. So, my past trials taught me to trust God with my finances, providing for me, peace, open doors, food, and shelter, paying my bills and watching my back against my enemies. But this battle was allowed to help me to trust God with my life!

I know I can't add a day or second to my life by worrying about it as stated in Matthew 6:27. I always wondered how I could see this scripture manifested in my life that says, "His perfect love casts out all fear." I am still waiting on this scripture to take me to new levels in my love of Christ. I'm still learning the power He has and the wisdom He can impart in our lives. I'm so thankful that His thoughts are not like our thoughts. Some battles we have to go through will be just you and God alone. I had to learn to stop being mad at people for not standing in the gap with me. In fact, I'm still learning this fact today. I have to let go of some ways and habits and allow God to have His way. I understand mental illness is a sickness that has unfortunately been swept under the rug for so long. It is looked upon with shame and it makes the individual feel worse. It can make people feel like they are a bother or shameful because of what you are going through, I take claims for some people who have anxiety, or they may have severe depression or bipolar, etc. They apologize so much for not remembering their information or just the shame they portrait during their appointment. I totally understand for the most part what they are going through and how they feel about themselves. I have a heart for anybody who is dealing with this illness or have done so in the past. Panic attacks are frightening! And you never know how it feels until you have gone through having them. They show up most times with little to no warning. To deal with panic attacks, I found myself taking deep breaths and focusing on where I was at the time. I would often just call someone who I knew could keep me calm until it passed. Depression keeps you frozen, you can't make any moves you want in your life because you are mentally tired and overwhelmed. The more you think about doing something the more tired you get. I would encourage myself with gospel songs or speaking aloud the promises of God over my life. The same God that did it then could do it for me now. I also would read scripture where I could see myself in what I was reading. It would confirm that what I was going through, was already defeated over 2000 years ago. I find that this has touched so many people that I know and love just by their actions. It takes a strong person to admit it and to say I need help. It takes an even stronger person to live with anxiety or depression and still function in life every day. The stigma keeps people from telling their truth.

Society, family or friends pass judgment and make you feel uncomfortable to share or ask for help. I'm telling my truth now because I know I am not alone in this battle. If I keep it to myself, then all my pain would have been in vain. I hope that by sharing my experiences and my truth I can help somebody along the way to live their best life. Anxiety was life-changing for me, it was bad and good. I know you're thinking, *how is anything good about anxiety Hope?* Let me tell you....

Anxiety taught me how to say NO when my plate was full and to not add anything else to it.

Anxiety taught me how to create boundaries and to speak up for myself in a way I never thought possible.

I mean, I tell MY truth whether the person wants to hear it or not. It made me angry enough to fight back against it and the hold it had on my life. Even if it doesn't completely go away, know that you have power over them all through Christ Jesus! Don't allow other's opinions of you to define you or your journey. But, like my pastor

Stephen E. Young Sr. says…. Keep living. You never know how you will handle or face these difficult times when they knock on your door unannounced.

As for me, I will not give in nor give up. Neither will you! I have dug my heels in and will continue to fight the good fight of faith. Nobody said the road would be easy, but we already have victory! The devil has already been defeated so you don't have to fight in your power. I am still learning to surrender and put it all on the altar and allow my God to have His way in my life. My goal is to create a platform where we can share and encourage each other daily. So, again I say Pardon Me, Post- You're defeated!!!

Overcoming the Battle with My Inner Critic

Written by Veronica L. Matthews

Come to me, all of you who are weary and carry
heavy burdens, and I will give you rest.
Matthew 11:28 NLT

*T*he first time my mother didn't recognize me, my heart sank, and I knew I had lost her. Although her body, her smile, and her loving eyes would remain on this earth for 6 more years, her mind and the mother I knew, no longer existed. Dementia would ravage her mind and diabetes would ravage her body making every day near torture for her. Dare I say all of my family as we all had some part to play in caring for her. Selfishly, I didn't want to let her go, so I prayed to God for her healing. So much so that one Sunday in church during alter prayer, my Pastor called me out and anointed my hands and told me to go straight to my mom to lay hands and pray over her. I did that, but nothing happened. I understood I had to have the faith that she would be healed and even she had to have the faith that she would be healed, and I believed we did, but still, there were no significant improvements... no lasting healing. Eventually, her health and mental faculties continued to decline, and my heart continued to break... slowly, until she passed on February 20,

2015, just two days after I started a new job. The timing couldn't have been worse. When all I wanted to do was curl up into a little ball and cry, I couldn't. Or I didn't believe I could. I had to hold it together, work, help with the arrangements and deal with the family drama that would come to the surface with my mother's passing. So, I avoided being with my feelings of grief, loss, loneliness, longing to talk to, hug, be with my mother.

Hindsight being 20/20, this was not the first time I recall avoiding and stuffing my feelings or listening to the voice inside. The first time was when I was 9 and was molested by an older neighbor, who I considered a friend. We were playing outside in another neighbor's back yard when he cornered me behind some sort of metal box in their yard. Hidden from view of others, he touched me between my legs. I froze. *What was he doing and what was happening,* were the thoughts running through my mind. My voice left me, my mind disconnected from my body and I recall him touching me, skin to skin – his fingers on my bare skin. I never had 'the talk' with my mom or dad, so I had no earthly idea what was happening. All I knew was it didn't feel right, I felt dirty and I was never able to look at him the same after that. It happened three other times before I found my voice to say that I didn't want that to happen anymore. I didn't tell anyone because I wondered what I did to make him want to do that to me. I hated him. I turned into myself, and I pushed down and aside from all the confusion, hurt and pain and did my best to move on. This was also the first time I recall listening to the voice inside – my inner critic who tried to protect me from someone finding out what happened.

I was raised Catholic and attended Catholic schools and although I knew who God was, I didn't have a relationship with Him. To me, prayer at that time was the Our Father and the Hail Mary. I had no concept of an open-hearted conversation with God to tell Him what I was feeling and experiencing. Shame had me not want to tell anyone what I was experiencing. So, stuffing it way deep down was my only option at the time and the voice inside confirmed that saying *don't say anything.*

Who I knew God to be changed in 1996 when I joined a Baptist Church in Richmond, VA and began eagerly cultivating a relationship with God through devotions, reading the Word and prayer. When my mother passed, I felt guilty that I didn't do all I could to help her through my faith in believing her to be healed and in caring for her. This led me to rally around my father. I grew closer to him, almost clung to him so he would feel my love in a way that I wasn't able to share with my mother.

Then, enter the family drama.

In the months following my mother's death, my father began 'hanging out' quite a bit. Unbeknownst to me, but known to my sisters, Dad began spending time with an old lady friend. This lady friend was the same woman who my father had a year's long affair with. I began to notice my father's decline mentally and physically, trying to burn the candle at both ends. The family drama was under the surface as I grew up, but I didn't want to believe that my hero and the smartest man in the world would hurt my mother and our family in that way. When his indiscretions resurfaced, I began to see my hero and the smartest man in the world differently. So, guess what? I suppressed my feelings and almost as tightly as I had clung to him before was the same extent to which I distanced myself from him. Yes, I visited and spoke to him regularly, but eventually, those visits and calls lessened with each passing week. The voice inside said, *'Call or visit him tomorrow; you've got time. You're too busy right now.*

Part of my father's decline was imbalance and an increased risk of falling. Well, fall he did in the shower after turning off the cold water and suffered 3rd-degree burns over much of his torso and groin area. He was hospitalized and, in my running, and avoidance, I didn't visit as often as my heart wanted to or I knew I should have. I had filled my life with so much busyness that I wasn't willing to make time for what was truly important. I just knew he would make it through and go home. I believed God that he would. However, as soon as I heard the news that the doctor's feared the end was near, I actually ran to something for a change. I got to the hospital as soon as I could. When I arrived at the burn ICU at Washington Hospital Center, they had me wait outside. Unfortunately, I knew why. In my transit, my father transitioned from this life – alone.

Talk about guilt, I missed him by 10 minutes!

Really, God... 10 minutes?!

I felt practically every negative emotion under the sun - heartbreak, anger, hurt, guilt that I wasn't there with him, frustration, disappointment, abandonment, and rejection. But what I felt most strongly was fear. I was a girl that loved her mommy and her daddy and had lost them both in two years and the fear that gripped me was breathtaking. The voice inside told me no one would understand your pain, so keep it to yourself. I believed no one would understand. Not even God.

So, true to fashion, I ran and avoided the heartbreak, the grief, the anger, the hurt, the guilt, the frustration, the disappointment, the abandonment, the rejection and most of all – the fear. I avoided it like the plague. "I'm okay," that was what I told myself and everyone else around me in the room during my coach training program the first weekend in December of 2017, the day after getting the news that I was terminated from my job. I'd been laid off before, but never terminated. And from a job I had only worked for nine months. I made a mistake out of fear, although I knew better and paid the ultimate price for it. I was as far from okay as someone, who was grieving and scared yet avoiding both the grief and the fear, could be. But I had to put on my big girl panties and move forward, right? At least that is what I told myself.

Instead of looking for another job, I poured myself into continuing to build my business. Unfortunately, the grief, fear, and my inner critic chased me down and corrupted my mind, self-esteem, self-confidence, hope, and belief in my capabilities that everything I tried was met with failure and one closed door after another. To make matters worse, I took on the responsibility of managing my father's estate. Yeah, right, who was I kidding? Although I wasn't working a 9-5 at the time, I had a full day of trying to get hired by clients to coach for income. The work of managing my father's estate was too much, so can you guess what I did, yep... I avoided it and only handled issues when it became an emergency and even sometimes when it was an emergency – like a foreclosure of the family home because of loan debt, I shut down completely instead of handling this major emergency.

With no steady income, my bills piled up and it was all I could do to pay the bare minimum – pay the mortgage, keep the lights on, the car note paid and gas in the car. Food was a luxury, but I didn't go to bed hungry for too many nights.

As a result, I spent the next six months running, hiding, listening to the voice inside that said act like everything is OK and it will be. I also spent the time isolating myself from not only the bill collectors but family, friends and particularly... God. Finally, the fear, pain, and pressure of the voice inside were so heavy that I cried out not even conscious that God was listening, but at the same time, hoping that he would hear....

"God! Where are you? What is going on? Why am I suffering like this?" His response spoke to my spirit, "Come to me, all of you who are weary and carry heavy burdens, and I will give you rest." Matthew 11:28 NLT

I was indeed weary (tired), carrying heavy burdens and in need of rest. I was tired of saying I was okay when I really wasn't; tired of hiding so I wouldn't have to answer the question of how and what I was doing; tired of avoiding all of the challenges I was facing; tired of struggling with the voice of my inner critic who constantly told me what I couldn't do; tired of wanting to hear my mommy and daddy's voices and not being able to. I was carrying heavy burdens – burdened with the guilt of not managing my responsibilities or the responsibilities of my father's estate;

burdened with major debt and more month than money; burdened with fear – the fear that my life would never get back on track and I would be stuck like this for the foreseeable future. Desperately in need of rest – although in my hiding I stayed in the house and slept a lot, it wasn't rest. Rest was a gift that I was not worthy of experiencing because I had ruined my life and gotten fired from a good job. Rest was a gift that I was not worthy of experiencing because I didn't feel worthy of anything good at the time.

In hearing God speak to my spirit, I realized that I had to get some help. I had to seek him and reignite that relationship that I was so excited to cultivate back in 1996. Fortunately, I had the wherewithal to apply for a part-time position and God blessed me to receive it. Through the job, I received benefits and was able to use medical insurance to receive support from a therapist. Through reconnecting with God and therapy, I was able to realize that I was suffering from depression and my avoidance was how the anxiety manifested itself. In hearing from God, I realized that while I distanced myself from God in shame, that he was still with me and loved me and wanted nothing but the best for me. Once I had time to look at my life, I realized that in the midst of my running that God was there all along and all I had to do was seek Him. He showed himself strong in that all the important bills got paid every month – the mortgage and the car note. I ate, maybe not steak and seafood, but I didn't miss too many meals; always had gas for my vehicle and money for the other essentials I needed. I never went without, God was and had always been my Jehovah Jireh, my Provider. The Holy Spirit helped me realize, in retrospect, that although I had been praying and reading my word, I was just going through the motions. I was not connected; I didn't have a true relationship. With true relationship, I would have been able to turn to God for help with my grief and fear instead of running from it. With a true relationship, I could allow God to fight the battle with my inner critic.

Through crying out to God, His answering and my receiving support, I was able to experience Matthew 11:29 NLT as Jesus spoke, "Take my yoke upon you. Let me teach you, because I am humble and gentle at heart and you will find rest for your souls." I returned to my first love – God and reconnected to God through prayer, reconnected to family and reconnected to my friends and support system. Spending real time with God through meditation on the word, devotion, and prayer and the support of my therapist, I slowly began to gain the strength and tools I needed to address the hard stuff – my grief, my debt, my depression, my anxiety, that negative voice in my head and my distance from God, family, and friends.

In this journey back to God, awakening and being still, I learned a few important strategies to help me bridge the gap from running away, avoiding my challenges and fighting the battle with my inner critic to standing flat-footed and facing them. While these points aren't new information, putting them together like puzzle pieces was necessary for me to gain the courage I needed to stop running, hiding and avoiding life's challenges.

1. **Foster a relationship with God to build faith, resilience, and strength to manage the everyday struggles of life.** Just like with any connection, relationship is built from spending time together, learning about each other and communicating. God doesn't need to learn anything about me, but I do need to not only learn but believe and have faith that the trinity (God, Jesus, and the Holy Spirit) are who

the Word says they are: Jehovah, Comforter, Chief Intercessor, Carrier of Burdens, Giver of Rest, My Glory and the Lifter Up of My Head and Provider of Peace. Through relationship, the experience of God became real for me to enable God to see me through my hurt and pain instead of dwelling in it.

2. **Stand in my truth and admit I needed help and accept the various types of help that was available.** The truth was, I needed help, more help than what I could give myself. James 4:2 NLT says, "You don't have what you want because you don't ask God for it." I had major needs, primarily, financial and emotional but shame and fear had me bound to silence and not asking God for what I wanted and needed. Once the Holy Spirit revealed to me that because of my relationship with God, I was free to ask, seek and knock and be blessed to receive, find and have doors opened for me. God showed me who I could ask for help and God used my family, friends, support system and opened doors of opportunity to provide the resources, emotional support, and

opportunities to allow me to come out from under the burdens, shame and avoidance to face my challenges through God and with support.

3. **Affirm who I am in God through God's Word to counterbalance the head trash from my inner critic that filled my head with self-doubt.** From the age of 9, I struggled with insecurities. Those insecurities came screaming back to me through negative self-talk that said you didn't do enough, you didn't love enough, you aren't good enough, you're stupid for making such a huge mistake, you're not capable of running a business, you're not a good Coach and so on, so on and so on. Negative thoughts ran through my mind on autopilot. One day in devotions, I heard the Spirit ask, "Who are you?" I was prompted to go through the Word to identify who I am in God and in God's eyes. I was awakened to who I am in God: more than a conqueror, victorious, loved, accepted in the beloved, the head and not the tail and so much more. I created affirmations that I used in the morning and throughout the day to remind me of who I

am in Christ and that helped to counterbalance the negative self-talk from my inner critic and resulted in a stronger self-belief and esteem.

I had established a pattern of stuffing my feelings, avoiding dealing with challenges that life threw my way and believing the voice of my inner critic. I had to understand that God was presenting these challenges to see my reaction, and would I turn to Him or away from Him. When I felt far from God, I was the one that moved. He was there all along standing ready and waiting to help me if only I would cultivate a relationship with him, stand in my truth to ask for what I needed and reinforced who I was in Him. I have forgiven myself for feeling like I failed; I'm closer to God; able to stand in my truth; affirmed of who I am in God and getting stronger financially and emotionally.

I realize now that I had to battle my inner critic who has consistently tried to get me to stifle my true voice and thoughts of who I am. In understanding who I really am in Christ, I, now, have a stronger relationship with God and knowledge of the Word to protect me, so the purpose of my inner critic has shifted and the voice I used to silence, now is free to speak and reaffirm who I really am. Today, she helps me to reject the thoughts that say otherwise. This has prepared me as a Coach, to empower women who struggle with the negative voice of their inner critic to transform the relationship within herself so the voice inside speaks to the truth of who she is in the Word of God and who she is destined to be. Whether my clients come to me seeking a career, interview, leadership development or executive coaching support, by God's design, somewhere in the process we discuss self-talk and their relationship to their inner critic. I've found this to be a foundational shift that is necessary to open the door to my client's true potential and destiny.

Today, I am so grateful to God for bringing me through, enabling me to overcome the battle with my inner critic, helping me to face my challenges and loving me all the while. Thank you, Lord; I love you.

Empowered to Overcome

Written by La Toya Braxton

"And the peace of God, which passeth all understanding, shall keep your hearts and minds through Christ Jesus."

Philippians 4:7

Being a survivor of child abuse, I have battled with and suffered from anxiety, depression, fear, insecurity, rejection, abandonment, low self-esteem, and post-traumatic stress disorder. Because of the abuse and rejection, it was always very hard for me to develop deep, lasting and trusting relationships and connections with others. So when people would reject me, I would feel the emotions attached to being rejected by my parents over and over again.

I wanted to be loved and accepted so bad that I became the ultimate people pleaser. Like the princess in Coming to America when Prince Akeem entered the room, my answer to almost anything asked of me was, "Whatever you like." I was willing to do whatever it took to keep people close to me from leaving, rejecting or abandoning me.

I would try my best to live up to other's expectations of me and some very unrealistic expectations I set for myself. Everything became very performance driven. Not only did I have to prove to others that I was worthy of being loved and accepted, I had to prove to myself that I was worthy of love and acceptance. I had never learned to love or accept myself, so I sabotaged relationships before I could get hurt. I wanted the relationships but if any of them triggered any memory of my abusive past, it was over.

Understanding Self-Love

To me, Self-love and Self-worth was about performance, accomplishments, achievements, awards, being the best and being at the top of my game. It was about making the most money, wearing the best clothes, driving the best cars and living in the best neighborhoods.

My performance, drive, and perfectionism became so intertwined with my personality and identity that when I wasn't able to meet the expectation and felt like I failed, I would fall into a deep depression. I would beat myself up and practice a lot of negative self-talk. I would feel insignificant, unworthy and useless. I needed a great deal of validation, affirmation, and encouragement to come out of my pity-party.

I couldn't handle the stress and anxiety of failure or things being out of control. Life as a child was so unpredictable and chaotic that I needed to be able to control everything in my life. Everything had to be predictable. If things did not go the way that I wanted them to go, I was gone; leaving a trail of wrecks behind me. Anything unpredictable or inconsistent with how I wanted my life had to be eliminated or replaced. That meant jobs, homes, church, family members, friends, and even my husband. I felt like I had already endured enough trauma and loss for a lifetime, and I was not willing to settle for anything less than perfect.

My life was like a roller coaster. Up and down depending on life's circumstances. Then one day, my life took a turn. God would prove to me that I was not the one in control of my life. I was working at a Christian Women's shelter and I was ready to answer the call of God on my life. I was hosting Bible studies, ministering to other women and boom! Their issues and testimonies began to trigger my issues and all of the trauma that I compartmentalized and hid. As a staff, we also had to attend training and group counseling and my entire ideal and delusional world was turned upside down. I began to relive every traumatic memory from my childhood, and I could no longer keep the idea of my life being perfect together.

My marriage was falling apart, I had post-partum depression, I was grieving the loss of my Goddaughter and a mentor, I had started going to therapy on my own and therapy was not working. I remember calling my Pastor, who was my Youth President at the time, and saying, "I need help! I don't understand what's going on!" And his words to me were, "You can't fight a spiritual battle naturally. The therapy isn't working because it's spiritual."

And without hesitation, in high anxiety and flight mode, I packed up my family and moved to Sacramento to begin a new life and a fresh start but, instead of things getting better, they became worse.

In the Midst of Transformation

I was now only in my marriage for my children, which resulted in infidelity, a bonus baby and separation. I experienced long periods of unemployment, we had now experienced homelessness more than three times. We lost everything we had, my health began to fail, my children were now experiencing depression and were in therapy. I received reports that my eldest son might be autistic and be at risk for testicular cancer and began experiencing extreme bouts of depression myself.

Once again, I found myself self-medicating through performance and busyness. Instead of dealing with the emotions and the reality of what was going on, I worked long hours at the church. I set no boundaries for others or myself. I became overinvolved in ministry until I was at the point of exhaustion and burn out.

I lived in total denial that my life was completely falling apart. My life became dark, isolated and broken. Even with all of the broken and shattered pieces lying out in the open, I still tried to present myself like I was a shiny, polished and well-put-together vessel. I had to prove to myself and others that I was strong, resilient, trustworthy, reliable and unbreakable not realizing that I had become the opposite of what I thought I was.

After the boys and I moved back with my grandmother, I was still operating in my old ways of being performance driven. I found myself being a single parent with little help and I was commuting from San Francisco to Sacramento to work and church, while also transporting the boys to school. I was stressed out trying to manage and balance it all.

Although I was very good at my job, being performance-driven wasn't working anymore. I showed up to work every day and cried and prayed at my desk in my cubicle. When I needed to cry hard, I would take a bathroom break. There was no denying that I was at my breaking point. Every day I would add a scripture to my cubicle wall to remind myself of what God said about me and who He said that I was. By the time my assignment was over, I had accumulated over 80 scriptures.

The Brim of Breakthrough

Everything seemed to be coming together. I found a job in San Francisco, transferred the boys to their new school, finally got my big boy an IEP with all of the services, he also had the surgery for testicular cancer, and I began to visit a church closer to home. While God was restoring everything that I had lost, I became ill three times in the same year. I never knew that those hospital admissions would change my life forever.

All three visits, no one outside of my family came to visit me. I was hurt, more broken, resentful, bitter and done! I was done with overextending myself, I was done with people-pleasing, I was done with meeting unrealistic expectations, I was done with trying to prove myself to others, I was done with loyalty, done with being performance driven, I was done with one-sided relationships, I was done with putting others before myself, I was done with trying to be in control of my life and I was done with me.

It was at this breaking point, in this brokenness, in this dark place and perceived rejection and abandonment that God began to deal with the root of rejection and I began to discover that the love, acceptance, and validation that I thought I needed from others, I really needed and only could get from God.

Once I finally acknowledged and accepted that I needed healing and deliverance to experience the freedom that I desired, I was able to authentically cry out to God for help. I needed a change. It was time for me to be honest and open with those closest to me about my "truths."

I wanted to totally surrender my life and my will to God with no fear, so I began to develop a deeper prayer and study life and committed myself to be better mentally, emotionally and spiritually.

A friend of mine referred me to a Christian counselor in the area to begin healing and unpacking all of the trauma that I had endured. I began to read books, practice self-care, positive self-affirmations, positive self-talk, invested in myself by gleaning from my coach, attending online workshops and classes and surrounding myself with positive role models.

The word of God and prayer are truly my mirror and my guide that I continually go back to when I begin to feel anxious or overwhelmed. I have adapted to and live by Philippians 4:6-8, "Be careful for nothing; but in everything by prayer and supplication with thanksgiving let your requests be made known unto God. And the peace of God, which passeth all understanding, shall keep your hearts and minds through Christ Jesus. Finally brethren, whatsoever things are honest, whatsoever things are just, whatsoever things are pure, whatsoever things are lovely, whatsoever things are of good report; if there be any virtue, and if there be any praise, think on these things."

Embracing Resilience

Pray until you get God's attention. In 1 Samuel chapter 1, Hannah put her petition before the Lord and wept bitterly. Scripture says that Hannah poured out her soul before the Lord, worshipped the Lord and the Lord remembered her. Your tears may be your meat day and night, but God honors your tears. Your tears coupled with faith, prayer, and worship will get God's attention. Even when people don't understand, don't feel like you have to move out of your broken posture until God answers.

While you are waiting, positive self-talk is so important. It's one thing to have others believe in you and for you but nothing will ever come of it if you do not believe for yourself. You have to have faith and believe even when your circumstances say something different.

Be honest with God and like the father in Mark 9:24, with tears in your eyes, cry out to God and tell him that you do believe but to help your unbelief. There is no use in pretending. We must worship Him, be vulnerable with Him and be honest with Him concerning where we are.

James 5:16; 19-20 focuses on accountability and healing. It's important to have healthy, nurturing and supportive relationships and community. These relationships are vital to your healing and growth. I have an amazing support system that loves me unconditionally, tells me the truth in love and prays for me continually.

Before you can overcome your struggles, you must be empowered to go through the process. Equip yourself with the tools and strategies that will help you stay committed to the process no matter what life throws your way.

From Pain to Purpose

Written by Misha-elle Hammer

"The LORD is near to those who have a broken heart, and saves such as have a contrite spirit."

Psalm 34:18

*H*ealing that comes from God is deep, priceless and lasting. By faith, I believe that God is going to heal you from any circumstance that has broken you. This chapter is my experiences with deep-rooted pain within and the triumph and healing the Holy Spirit gave me and my family.

When I was young, I remember loving my father passionately. I remember sitting on his knee bouncing up and down. I remember being placed on his feet, belly touching the bottom of his heels and being lifted in the air as I tried to desperately balance, hands interlocked with his holding on for dear life. This love went deep. Daughter to Father and Father to Daughter. Our family was intact. Me and my older sister would travel to school together and back home. Things were right. Our house was safe, and it FELT safe. That would change when I became a second-grader.

The love me and my father shared would be tested, broken, changed, diminished, effected by the trials of his life and ultimately leaving a lasting and wounding impact on me. Before I tell you of my father's struggles, I want to describe the father I loved. My father migrated from Nicaragua in hopes to prosper in America. He was a fit man. He enjoyed exercise, sports, and family. He took care of his wife and his children. He loved God and studied religious teachings. He was optimistic about life. He was a treasure. By the age of 22, he became a husband, at the age of 23 he had his first child, and by the age of 31 he became an alcoholic and at 55, he passed away from cancer.

As a daughter, you do what Mommy says. I was 5, and that day I learned something new. I learned a lesson on concealing. What does a person do when they do not want anybody to find out about their actions? What does a person do when their actions will be scrutinized, brought into judgment and frowned upon? Most people will hide and conceal these matters from others. It was true with my father.

I had come into my mother's room as I saw her pulling out a clear bottle full of clear liquid lodged under the bedframe. I thought to myself, *who on earth would put a full bottle under the bed and why is Mommy acting so upset about finding a full bottle of clear juice?* My young mind only comprehended that it was something my mother did not approve of. When she took the bottle to the bathroom sink and poured out all of its' content, it became clear to me of her disapproval. Looking back on things, I now know what it was, it was a bottle of vodka. That moment changed my home dynamics. From that point on, my father's battle with alcoholism had come to the forefront, even me, his baby girl, now had eyes that were getting a glimpse of his pain.

Recognizing Generational Curses

God is a good God and he exposes sin to reveal our need for repentance and gives us an opportunity for us to receive His grace and mercy. Often, however, the exposure is just an indicator for others to see the battle that is being fought for that person's soul, which began well before the outward exposure takes place. Exposure can do two things for people, it can cause them to receive God's grace or it can cause them to go into an out of control spiral, causing the sin they find themselves in to take full control of their lives. In my father's case, sin took control of his life causing him to become an alcoholic.

When I first began going to church, I would hear teachings about generational curses. I did not know what they were until God opened my eyes to my own family's generational curses. I can tell you they are real and curses on families are the same throughout the generations. Generational curses are not easily won, however, they are defeated only by the blood of Jesus. I can also tell you that God always has a chosen person/s that He chooses to demolish the curses that plague our families. My family's generational curses are addiction and domestic violence. My father had them both.

I was asleep with my sister and mother in the bed. I don't remember doing this very often as a child, so I recall this memory very vividly. In hindsight, I realize that my mother had purposefully put us in her bed that night. I was 5, my sister was 7. I woke up to a scream, "Neil no!" I heard my mother pleading with my father to stop whatever he was doing. I perched myself up in the bed to see what the commotion was about. At the edge of the bed, I saw my father trying to overpower my mother. She was pushing him off her. I then saw his hand raise and fall hard down upon my mother. All I could think at that time was, *my mother is pregnant, please don't let Dad hit my mom in her stomach, I want the baby to live.*

My father would not stop, and I grew more and more afraid. As fear began to consume me and my older sister, we curled up at the corner of the bed. As I was living what would later be identified as trauma in my life, my feelings of fear began to change. My feelings changed from fear to rage.

At 5 years old, I began my first battles with anger, frustration, and rage. These battles would continue well into my adult years, hindering me with bad attitudes that would contend with my open doors and blessings that should otherwise flow into my life. What I remember so vividly was being so enraged with my father for what he was doing to my mother, I wanted to run to the end of the bed and hit him as hard as I could to get him to stop. As a young 5-year-old, one's idea of strength is not grounded in reality. As I plotted on what type of force could take down my father, I began to experience a different emotion. It was fear. Suddenly, I had no more courage, rather all I had was fear. Fear for my mother, fear for myself. The world changed for me that day. I realized something for the first time. I realized I was not covered and that harmful events along with evil spirits lurked in my home. I was no longer safe.

I would experience many forms of being unsafe in my life. Several times, I should have gotten seriously affected by either my choices or the bad choices of others around me. I know what it is like to fear for your life while being strangled. I know what it is like to be completely unprotected in forms of bullying and manipulation. I have felt the sting of fear from the demonic presences that came at night to the manifestation of those same spirits. I've experienced a lot. I have been through so much. But I have been saved by God's grace and love. I have been healed by His spirit. And I know God wants the same for you, too. God wants to take the traumatic experiences you have had that have left you shattered within and heal you.

Revealing the Spirit of Satan

Destroying your soul is not possible by the enemy. Satan does not have this type of power. Thank God! The only thing Satan can do is afflict us. Meaning, Satan can only cause harm and cause foul but never destroy your eternal soul. The pain that is in your life is an affliction.

An affliction wound's you. An affliction takes from you. An affliction doesn't go away. And an affliction is categorized as light in the Bible. 2 Corinthians 4:17 says, "For our light affliction, which is but for a moment, worketh for us a far more exceeding and eternal weight of glory." Have you ever asked yourself why does God's word call afflictions, light afflictions? Light afflictions come to torment us but never to destroy us.

The pain that you are feeling is a light affliction in God's eyes. Not because it is marginalized, general, or meaningless. It is light because compared to God's ability to avenge and take care of us is far greater than the affliction that has found its way into your soul.

Now we must realize that the human spirit and soul are a supernatural existence. Therefore, when pain exists in these places, the remedy, the healing balm, the answers, and the direction must come from the supernatural. If it were our bodies that needed healing, those answers are grounded and treated by natural remedies. When our souls have been fractured and our spirits have been broken, these wounds can only be healed by the Spirit of God.

The Spirit of God works with the spiritual indwelling of Jesus the Lord within our hearts to bring about true, divine and inspired healing. He can heal the molestation you went through, the betrayal you suffered in, the mistreatment from others.

When I was young, I had a reoccurring dream. The dream was me in a cage yelling for my dad to come let me out and help me while short demon-like creatures would be dancing around me, chanting and celebrating that they had caught me in their cage. Looking back, this is what I was living in. I was living in a house full of turmoil and an evil presence. My mother is a loving individual, her actions were not the cause or the source Satan used. Unfortunately, all Satan needs to accomplish his plan is one person. Satan preys on people, he successfully finds wounded souls, weakened faith, generational curses and God-haters to work his plans. The enemy had entered into my home not because of myself, rather because of the actions of others.

I experienced many broken relationships of all sorts as I would grow up. It wasn't until I was 22 years old that I realized the source of my brokenness stemmed from my relationship with my father. You see, it was Satan's plan all along to get me bound from infancy. The demons I would dream about became real. They manifested in real-life situations that kept me out of God's will, grace and love. The demons constantly set up situations where I would seemingly be bound. Where do you see the first signs of going astray from God? Was it in your childhood? Was it in your teens? I know it was somewhere because when we are led by God and in His will, He protects us. Psalm 91 states, "When we are outside of God's protection, the enemy sends traps that will take our lives to destruction, hurt, turmoil and pain." It is never God's will to bring pain into our lives. God is a loving God, willing to give us a life full of joy, abundant blessings and increase. This means that God desires for us to be our best selves. He wants to see us flourishing and being successful in this world. His desire for you is to bless you and love you. Satan desires to hurt you, to kill you, to tear your life in pieces so that you can no longer see God's will, plan or blessings upon your life.

I suffered in my household spiritual turmoil pretty much my entire childhood. Please don't read into this wrong. I had a loving mother and a loving father, however, my father was an alcoholic and I am convinced, without proof, that he was involved in some type of occult. The spirits that were at work in my house were spirits resistant to God, evil and with ill intent.

God would later use this early exposure to the spirit realm. Before I was saved by God's grace, I possessed a knowledge of the spirit world that was unexplained or unexplored in my life. I am convinced that God had his hand upon me so that I did not get drawn into occult practices, tarot readings or witchcraft. They allured me pretty deeply. I knew of things that were not disclosed to me personally. Later, I would learn to use and operate in the prophetic gifting as I would accept my calling to serve the Lord.

During these days, however, I attracted a lot of evil spirits in my life. I have learned that with spiritual giftings from the Lord, you must be prepared to handle the revelation of not only heaven but of hell as well. Spirits need humans to operate their will on this earth. They afflict you in many ways. Demons are at the root of a lot of pain and misfortune. Although God has revealed the spirit world to me, I remain in complete surrender to God's Spirit as he reveals things of evil.

Disguised Devils

When I was in 2nd grade we moved to Spokane, WA. From this point on, my father was no longer an active or permanent member of my household. Although shortly after we moved to Spokane, my father quit drinking. Even though he stopped drinking he never really recovered all the way. His life was still very broken. My mother and my father bickered and argued often. I grew up in this type of household throughout my high school years. My memories of my father in Spokane are extremely limited. After a few years of living in Washington, my father relocated from California. He lived in Spokane but did not live in our home. He would go "home" to his separate residence which was an apartment located downtown. Because of the ongoing absence of my father, I grew to think I did not really need my father. I grew up with my mother, did well in school, advanced in my pursuits of life. It wasn't until God opened my eyes in my early 20's to the impact of my fatherless life. Before God opened my eyes, I would make terrible choices and continue making terrible choices in men because of my fatherless upbringing.

I began to have relationships with the opposite sex early in my life. By the time I was 16 years old I was dating a 26-year-old drug dealer. I now ask myself, *why on earth was I dating such a terrible person?* I blame it on ignorance. I was ignorant of who I was to become in Christ. Without our identity, worth and purpose grounded only in Christ we will suffer loss in different areas. My area of loss was in relationships. Not only would I attract abusive men, but I would also suffer at their forms of violence, betrayal, self-absorption, and lack of spirituality. If you can relate, you too must identify where this pattern has begun in your life.

We cannot control what other people do, but we can control what choices we make. When I did not have a revelation on just how deeply I had been affected by my father's absence, I was vulnerable to making bad decisions, simply based on what I did not have or know. I had a father, but I didn't have a shepherd. I had a father, but I didn't have a protector. I had a father, but I didn't have a leader. I had a father, but I did not have his loving presence. The lack of the Godly relational content between a father and daughter, originally intended by God, had been stolen from me by sin and Satan. Me not having the necessary care made me prey for some predators and hopelessly vulnerable to my own ignorance.

Deliverance Ignited

There are three significant choices in men that God used to show me my condition and ultimately deliver me from such bondage. These relationships were abusive physically, mentally, emotionally and spiritually. These relationships all started with a bang but ended in extreme disappointment and I was worse off than ever before.

Physically abusive men never announce their problems to you in the beginning. They wait until the right time to pounce on you, literally. The right time for them looks like when you are in love with them, making the grip and hold they have on you incredibly hard to break. It wasn't until I was dragged on the floor, threatened with an object and forced to call the police that I safely ended my abuser's torment in my life.

We had just got done hanging out from what I would describe as a fun-filled night out. When he asked me why I let that guy lean into my ear and tell me something, I had no idea it was a set up for the beginning of his physical abuse. I answered the question with as much innocence and ignorance I had that night. The answer was simple, I said, "Because he had something to tell me about you." Honestly, the guy had something good to say about him, but my abuser did not care. He wanted to establish dominance that night. When I gave my answer, I was met with a hard slap to my right cheek. I was in shock. I would have never thought that he would hit me. I would have never thought I would be the one getting hit like I saw my mother getting hit. I sat in disbelief, stunned by the startling and hurtful slap. In those moments all I could do was relive my childhood trauma of my drunk father coming into my mother's room that night. I too was living out the terrible experience that shaped my childhood years with my father and mother. I too had gotten hit. I too was in fear. I COULD NOT BELIEVE this was happening to ME. Well, it did, and it kept happening, despite the promise he made that night to never hit me again.

It wasn't until I cried out to God for deliverance from this abusive relationship did, I see any change. Domestic violence does not end until the victim gets out of that relationship. As a victim myself, I can say, that it is not easy getting out of abusive relationships. There is always this desire and hope for the one causing harm, to change. The only thing that changed was my sanity, my peace, my physical appearances, my mind, my life, my money, my job, my sin, and my life experience. I now had experienced intense trauma that would take years for me to recover from.

The intent was set from the Devil to destroy me, physically, mentally and spiritually. This evil intended attack did not begin with my abusive relationship, it began with my father's lineage. It began with the generational curse, it began the night of my father's attack on my mother, it began in heaven with God and Satan. However, it did not end there.

The Bible tells us that we overcome by the Blood of the Lamb and the word of our testimony. If it had not been for my relationship with God and my knowledge of crying out to Him for deliverance, I would not be delivered and set free from an abusive spirit in my life.

Crying out to God is from the heart. When we make our requests and desires known to God, He will listen and be true to His word. The Bible tells us, "seek God with your whole heart while He may be found..." Finding myself in such a terrible situation was heartbreaking and dangerous. At that time, I needed deliverance. You too may need deliverance from a terrible situation. I want to share with you some practical steps you can take if you find yourself in need of deliverance of any kind.

First, repent. Repentance is our first step in deliverance. Our relationship with God exists in the heart. Most sins come from the wickedness of our hearts. Although you may not be the one causing the situation to become broken, you have a part in the entire situation. Therefore, as a believer, because you have access to God, repent before Him. The Bible says if we confess our sins, He is just to forgive us and cleanse us. When I got revelation about this scripture, the cleansing part is what jumped out at me. With all the turmoil and trauma I experienced from my father's and my relationship and now an abusive man, I needed an ample amount of cleansing. The moment I began to experience trauma, I was not the same person. You won't be either. When you have experienced trauma you need healing, cleansing, releasing and purifying. That's what our relationship with God does for us.

As I grew up without a father I would get into relationships with different men for different reasons. I had reasons that compile a long list.

Some reasons I would get involved with men were boredom, control, love, attention, and sex. It never was for the reasons God reveals in his word. It was never for the service of my mate, for the love of God's sons or the procreation of family. It was always rooted in my own selfish needs. As I look back on these relationships and their many different reasons, I can find the root cause to be my broken relationship with my father.

I sit writing this book as a woman surrendered to God as His servant. I sit as now a wiser, educated, prayerful and woman of substance, strength, and power in God's kingdom. I can truly say, God has redeemed the time in my life. All that I have lost, or has been stolen from me, I have regained in my identity in the Lord. Before I received my redemption, God had to heal me. God had to show me the areas of my life and the root cause of my turmoil, my anger, my searching, my brokenness. You too have been chosen for God's healing. You too have been chosen to go deep to the root of your pain and pull it up at its root. What a blessing it is for God to do such amazing things in our lives. Do not take it lightly the wonderful gift of healing Jesus has decided to give to you.

Whether you can testify now or later, you will be healed by the power and faithfulness of our God.

Deliverance began in my life during my years at the School of Urban Missions Bible College in Oakland, California. I had been saved two years before my deliverance truly began. I was attending church and experiencing God on a corporate level, it was now time to experience God on a personal level. He began with my father.

Redeem Me Oh Lord

God began to show me just how much I had been negatively affected by my broken and absent relationship with my father. After all these years of not having him as a sturdy focused and dependable father, I was brought back to the realities of his actions in my life. The Lord began to reveal to me that I had been affected so deeply that I could no longer see the impacts it had on my life. When we have consistent and ongoing situations in our life, at times, we can begin to simply accept these situations as normal, as just the way things are. As Christians, we know that situations God creates in our lives are good, they are full, they are perfect. The Psalm writer writes "As for God, His ways are perfect."

God had begun to show me that not having a father in my life slowly and surely changed me into an image unlike Christ's true intent for me. God began to show me that I had become extremely distrustful toward men, so distrustful I put up a wall of self-defense. This wall existed in the form of control, or what I thought was control over the men I chose to be with. This way of thinking took me to places in my heart and mind that God had to deliver me out of. This effect took deep root into my life and had to be uprooted by the power of God.

Expectation in a relationship turned inwardly to how was I going to receive God's blessings in the midst of a situation where the person was not changing. I began to take on my role as a daughter instead of criticizing the role that I was not held accountable for.

When my father was 55 years old, he would get diagnosed with stomach cancer. I remember the day he died. When I got the call, I was pumping gas. I answered the phone and heard my mother's voice tell me my father had passed. It was like the earth went silent and I stood in that reality and felt the sting of his death.

Nothing prepares you for losing a parent. The wound stays open for a while and feels like a hole in your spirit with nothing to fill it.

Before my father passed away, I came to visit him. His room was quiet, and he lay on the bed when I came in. I asked my father how he was doing. He was able to say he was doing well and that he was sorry for all the disappointments he had brought into me and my siblings' life. I had forgiven my father years before and I was happy for him to ask for forgiveness. This showed me that my father's heart was getting worked on. Prior to that, my father was honery, negative, accusatory and stubborn. I knew that God was working on him. I took full advantage of that moment. I asked my father if I could pray for him. Without hesitation, he answered yes. All the years before when I would talk about God to my father, I was met with a staunch attitude or dismissed with irrelevance in his eyes. This day, his heart was ready. I asked, "What are we going to be asking God for?" He said, "healing." Honestly, I was surprised that my father wanted anything from God. I knew it was his time to mend his broken relationship with God. I also knew that all of his pain that effected his loved ones, his family, his ambitions were because he had renounced his relationship with God. It filled my heart with adoration that God was still there waiting for my father to cry out to him once again and be reunited with his heavenly Father's embrace.

It happened all in front of my eyes. God had never left my father. God suffered right alongside him all those years. Through his addiction, broken relationships, emotional pain, cancer, resentment, unhappiness, unfulfillment, God was still there. As I took the prayer oil and anointed his body and prayed for healing, the Lord showed me that my father needed emotional healing as well as physical healing. They were tied together, connected by the pain his soul had endured. At that moment, the Holy Spirit entered the room and he led me to tell my father what God wanted from him. I said to my father, "I sense that God wants you to say Thank You to Him." He paused for a little while and then he said it, he said: "Thank You." I sat in silence with this moment as he had begun to open his spirit back up to his heavenly father. And then I heard it again from his loins, from his unction, from his direction, "Thank You." The second thank you came from his testimony, his own once broken relationship with God to now a reconciled reverence and gratefulness to his Creator. I knew that my father had just released years and years of pain in that one moment. I knew that God had healed him emotionally and physically in that one moment. Our God is amazing, thank you, Lord Jesus.

My father would pass a few weeks later while reconciled with my mother, his wife, in her home with the rest of my siblings. After my father's passing, I inquired of the Lord the meaning of the healing he performed on my father. In God's way, He let me know that He did indeed heal my father's body by taking him into His glory, God was able to give him a new body, a new spirit, a new heart and a new mind in heaven. All the years of suffering my father endured on earth was healed in an instant and because my father reconciled with God before he passed away, he was now experiencing eternal life, free from emotional pain, physical pain and passed mistakes he had made.

Purposeful Empowerment

As for me, yes, I was affected. Yes, I was affected by my father's bad choices, but through that, God opened my eyes to my eternal deliverance. I did not have to wait until I got to heaven to experience complete healing. God wanted to heal me now, here, on earth. He did not cause my bad choices in men, but he delivered me out of bad choices in men forever. Because of His deliverance, I can come up against generational curses and command them to flee from my life, flee from my family and have dominion over these demons whenever I pray for others experiencing such turmoil.

God does not cause pain in our lives but, He is the only one that can heal the pain that is in our lives. Because we have God, we can overcome the obstacles of shame, curses, negativity, bondage, and anything that is keeping us from the abundant life Jesus has for us. If you are experiencing pain from other people's bad choices around you, you must know that God can heal you from that. The promise is not to change the other person or have them come to realize their wrongs. The promise is for you and your pain to be resolved.

- **Psalm 147:3** says, "He heals the brokenhearted and binds up their wounds."

- **Psalm 126:5** says, "Those who sow in tears Shall reap in joy."

- **Psalm 34:18** says, "The LORD *is* near to those who have a broken heart and saves such as have a contrite spirit."

All these scriptures spoke life into me when I faced emotional pain. If I did not have the promise that God would wipe away all my tears, I would not have hope to face my disappointments. The scriptures tell us to cling to what is good, God is good. His word is good. His promises are good. His faithfulness is dependable. His riches are truly unsearchable. And his understanding, incomparable. I know that God can heal, and I know that God can and wants to heal you.

You are the reason I wrote this chapter.

You are the reason I opened myself up to write a book.

God wants you to know that the pain that is rooted deep down inside can be brought to the surface and healed. We have to bring that pain to Him. You may ask, how? How do I bring this pain to God?

Second, it is in prayer. If we do not intentionally set our hearts and minds to having God fix our pain, we will find ourselves suffering in our sins and our coping mechanisms again, much like I was when I was in my abusive relationships.

Identify that you need God to heal you. When God heals us from deep-rooted pains, it happens with time and in parts. When the pain can be traced back to childhood, it will take experiences with God to bring your full and promised healing into your heart. God uses friendships, jobs, churches, broken relationships, failures, mistakes and pain to help us identify that we need God's healing in our lives. Those experiences that have left you hurt, frustrated and disappointed have the greatest potential in your life to bring you closer and much more aware of God's hand, presence and work in your life. Without the pain, you would not have to cry out to him.

Cry out to God. Cry with the brokenness, confusion, resentment and all. Bring all of that part of you to prayer. Cry from a real place. Open your heart to God. Open your mouth and speak to God. Tell God what you want most of all in your pain. Ask God to renew that part of your life. Ask God to free you from generational curses. Ask God to free you from the pain within. When God begins to heal you, forgive those that have offended you. Forgive with Jesus forgiveness, after all, they too are sinners needing a savior. Your healing is a prayer away, a cry away, a tear away, a forgiveness away, a day away. God is faithful and he WILL heal you, set you free and give you a testimony. You belong to the beloved. He is not a respecter of persons. What he has done for me, He will do for you. I stand with you. I hold your hands up. I point you to your savior. I encourage you. I speak life into you. You will conquer, you will overcome, you will glorify God in your testimony. Magnify the Lord with me, exalt His name, praise Him for what He has done for you and what He is going to do for you.

Begin to thank him, like my father began to thank him. Even in his frailty, his death bed, God was faithful to him. God met my father where he was at and gave him his eternal healing. Keep pressing in God's presence. God completely healed my father emotional and physically in His own timing and in his own way. Maybe it is not on your death bed, but it is now that God is meeting you where you are at. Maybe it won't take an illness to bring you to His arms of healing but, it is taking your experiences that have left you in pain to bring you to Himself eternally. God is going to finish the work he began in you. He began his work in my life at 19 years old. He has been relentless with his love for me, deliverance I need and emotional wholeness he desired for me since the beginning of the world. I have had to figure out the hard way that God loves me, but I DID figure it out. It was His love that took me from that abusive man, false friends, judgmental people and more. It is only because He loves me that He uses my experiences to bring me closer to Himself and His kingdom. His love has brought me out of situations that were meant to leave me broken, confused, abused and forgotten. But his love, his love, his love is everlasting, overcoming, higher and sharper than anything you or I will face in this world.

So I say to you, look up, look to the hills, look to God, look to his everlasting kingdom, his eternal purposes, and His love. This direction will bring you up, out, delivered, set free and ultimately heal and whole. God bless you. I love you in Jesus.

About the Authors

Jessica LeeAnn - Visionary

Jessica LeeAnn is called to empower women of Faith to build a strong relationship with God to live a purpose-driven & abundant life. Having experienced many seasons of being a Prodigal Daughter, Jessica answered the call from God while sitting in the back of a cab in 2012. Broken and uncertain, Jessica gave God her "Yes" and have embarked on a quest to rebuild her relationship with God, boldly pursue her purpose, as well as empower other women who are lost and broken to do the same. As the visionary of *Qualified to Reign*, Jessica gives God glory for the vision, platform, & women apart of this project.

Angela Robertson

Angela Robertson was born in New Orleans, LA and raised in Oakland, CA. She is a Wife, Mom, Behavior Analyst Student, Author and Empowerment Speaker. Angela loves to help people understand how to live their best life through the teachings of faith-based content.

Chelle Keith

Chelle Keith was born June 3, 1971 in Welch, WV; the youngest of nine siblings. After beating medical odds as an infant by the grace of God, she grew to be known in the community for being blessed with the gift of song throughout the different churches. She is currently serving as an Evangelist in the church founded by her late mother, Elder Rosetta Keith.

Callandra Smith

Callandra Smith is an author and a creative who creates items and resources that uplift, empower, and encourage others throughout various phases of their life's journey. Her faith-based content helps to enrich women in the areas of confidence and hope. In this book, she illustrates that cultivating a life of joy and meaning and moving out of a place of hopelessness and despair are possible.

Hope Marr

Hope Marr is an Author and Empowerment Speaker. She aspires to create a line of Encouragement Journals to help women track their journey to victory! She loves giving God praise and has a heart for anyone who has suffered at the hand of anxiety, depression, fear and postpartum. Her desire is to inspire and help others overcome this mental illness by using the word of God and faith.

Veronica Matthews

Veronica L. Matthews is an accomplished and certified Coach, Human Resources Consultant, Author, Public Speaker, Trainer and Workshop Facilitator. She is a native of Prince George's County, Maryland and a cum laude graduate of Howard University. She is fulfilling her purpose to successfully coach her clients to get out of their own way to create lives they love and fulfill their greatest potential. Additionally, Veronica provides coaching, training and HR Consulting services to start-up and small businesses in need of quality HR, leadership and professional development support.

La Toya Braxton

La Toya Braxton is a native and emancipated foster youth of San Francisco, CA. Her passion for young women has driven her to teach and mentor young ladies through the Young Women of Excellence Program, the San Francisco Independent Living Skills Program and the Community College Foundation, which both serve current and former foster care youth, and the Shepherd's Gate Christian Shelter, whose mission is to free women and children from the destructive cycles of homelessness, addiction and abuse. La Toya strongly believes that sharing and demonstrating the authentic love of Jesus Christ through mentoring can empower young ladies to overcome the effects of childhood trauma to break negative cycles, habits, and thinking.

Misha-elle Hammer

Misha-elle (Misha) Hammer was called into God's ministry at the age of 19. Sensing the unique call of God on her life, she pursued and finished her Master's degree in Theology from Fuller Theological Seminary. Misha has spoken to many of God's children in conferences and churches. God uses the prophetic mantle on her life to release blessings, victories and the fire of God in His children's lives. Her hope and prayer for you is that you will embrace God's unique design and call upon your life while walking in the blessings and liberty God gives to you. She is most grateful when she is used in other's lives to point them to the way of their Savior, Jesus our Lord.

Made in the USA
Middletown, DE
28 February 2020